Strong Fathers,
Strong Children,
Strong Families,
and
Strong Communities

Published in the United States by
Beckham Publications Group, Inc.

ISBN: 0-931761-62-X
10 9 8 7 6 5 4 3 2 1

Library of Congress Cataloging-in-publication data: 2007941421

Strong Fathers, Strong Children, Strong Families, and Strong Communities

A Guide for Responsible Fatherhood

Dr. Willie L. Barber

THE Beckham
PUBLICATIONS GROUP, INC.

Silver Spring

CONTENTS

Pioneers in the Fatherhood Movement

I dedicate this book to all fathers, especially those who have participated in a responsible fatherhood program. I also dedicate it to the following, whom I have met or worked with and consider to be dedicated, compassionate, and pioneers in the "Responsible Fatherhood Movement:" Dr. Ron Mincey, Dr. Jeff Johnson, Joe Jones, Ed Pitt, Stanley Bernard, Alvin Collins, the late Ken Wilson, Don Christian, Sheridan Stanley, Charles Ballard, Anthony Williams, Johnny Rice II, Lonnie Perrin, Leon Henry, D. J. Andrews, Dr. Wade Horn, Tyrone Stokes, Avon Bellamy, Donald Malcom Smith, Ademola Ekulona, Richard Rowe, David Miller, Dr. Vivian Gadsden, Steve Rhode, Steve Lawrence, Dr. Yolanda Abel, Leon Purnell, Londell Owens, Theodora Ooms, Darryl Green, Erick Brinner, James Worthy II, William and Stacie Hall, Alvin Parks, Preston Garrison, David Bordley, Pastor Marvin McFadden, and Charles "Skip" McDaniels.

FOREWORD

Thank God for Dr. Willie Barber. He blessed fathers—several years ago—with the powerful, melodious, finger-popping and toe tapping CD, *Responsible Fatherhood* that not only recaptured, reclaimed and reaffirmed the blessed and sacred role of fatherhood, but his CD also encouraged and inspired fathers not to abdicate their responsibilities, to strive to become exceptional fathers, and to celebrate, whenever possible, those men in the community that take their role as fathers seriously. While we should be encouraged by the number of fathers who have accepted the challenge to connect with their children in recent years, there are still far too many fathers that are not connected to their children and are spending far too much time "hanging" with the boys, watching television, or making excuses for not being able to make it to open houses, PTA meetings, dance recitals, karate lessons, the museum, or the church. Those fathers must be reached and they must be reached immediately. At a time when black families—especially black children—are under siege by a pop culture that promotes and defends the highest levels of confusion and hedonism, black fathers must return home to reclaim their families and their communities.

So, how do we reach those fathers that are missing in action? What can we say to them that will bring them back to their children and their communities? What structures and programs are needed to support the fathers who are desirous of assuming their sacred role as caring and committed fathers? What is the impact of fatherlessness on children—both girls and boys? How do we serve and support those fathers that are incarcerated, and those who have been released from prison? What strategies are needed to strengthen the relationship between fathers and the children's mother? What about grandfathers and grandchildren? When it comes to enhancing parenting and conflict mediation skills, are there best practices that should be adhered to by programs working with fathers? How should we approach the spiritual, physical and psychological health of fathers? What role does government play in supporting fathers and what supportive role must the community assume?

Again, thank God for Dr. Willie Barber. His new contribution, *Strong Fathers, Strong Children Strong Families, and Strong Communities*, is an insightful, illuminating and instructive guide that not only addresses many of the essential questions, but it also provides critical advice and support for fathers and those individuals working with fathers. Dr. Barber understands that being a father is the most sacred and important role a black man will ever, ever hold and it cannot be taken lightly. In an increasingly dangerous and unpredictable world, the absence of positive, caring and nurturing fathers adds tremendously to the insecurity of children and to the rise in both family and community instability.

His book, like his CD, encourages total involvement of fathers with their children. His book is designed to move all of us beyond rhetoric, marches and task force studies. His book sets a clear path for fathers that will move them to the ultimate conclusion: that they owe their children, families and communities their love, time, prayers, leadership and protection. The take-away message from this very important work is that fathers must stop bemoaning the things that are done to them and focus on the things they can do for themselves. Fathers are not powerless! They must rise to the occasion and return home—both spiritually and metaphysically—to restore their families, rescue their children and reclaim their communities.

Brother Barber is urging all fathers to "father up" and to join forces with other serious, sober, spiritual and selfless men to seize the opportunities of the future, reclaim the lessons of the past, and become the examples of fatherhood needed to guide their children into responsible adolescence and adulthood. It is very clear to Dr. Barber that the mothers of the village cannot and should not have to raise the children by themselves. And even though many of them will try, it is a losing battle without cadres of caring, courageous and committed fathers in the village stepping up and assuming their roles as fathers.

This book takes a strong stand on the issue of responsible fatherhood. Given Dr. Barber's exemplary example as a father, practitioner, gifted musician, community activist and educator par excellence, this guide should be read by everyone who believes we are the salvation of us. If not us, then who! Thank God for Brother Barber!

—Richard A. Rowe, Founder of the Leadership Circle and President/CEO of the African-American Male Leadership Institute

Introduction

I dedicate this book to my father, the late Jay Shannon Barber, Sr. and to the many fathers I have known who have recognized and demonstrated the important role that fathers play in the lives of their children and families. I also want to recognize the many young men I have met who did not have a responsible father in their lives—those who reside in group homes, receive services through outpatient mental health programs, attend public schools, attend church, and participate in community-based programs.

I sincerely hope that this book will assist these young men and others, who will either become or are already fathers, to be the best responsible, committed, and available father they can be for the benefit of their children and their children's children for generations to come.

Originally, my message was to be directed toward African-American urban fathers. I wanted to help them understand the important role they play in the growth and development of their children. As the book developed, I realized that it would have value not only for African-American and other minority fathers in urban communities, but also for all fathers—regardless of race, culture, socio-economic status, and religious affiliation. Finally, I also want to reach those fathers who are indeed fulfilling their roles and responsibilities. They too can benefit by gaining additional skills and learning new strategies that are designed to improve their relationships with their children.

We have a grave problem facing our nation: too few fathers are in the homes and in the lives of our children. Some fathers are actually in the homes—physically, that is, but not emotionally. The crux of the matter is that too many fathers do not understand the significant roles they play in the growth and development of their children. They don't see the long-standing negative impact that an uninvolved father has on a child. Of course, many fathers have grown up without a father in the home or a significant positive role model in their lives. That personal history has a major impact on how they perform their parenting roles and responsibilities.

Nevertheless, it's time for a wake-up call for responsible fatherhood.

I sincerely hope that this book will be that call— a crying out to fathers and future fathers to understand their roles in the growth and development of their children and recognize the damaging impact that the lack of an involved father can have on a child.

I have drawn from many readings; direct contact with fathers, children and families; and conferences. I also call upon my experiences as the first statewide director of Responsible Fatherhood Programs for the State of Maryland and, more importantly, of being the father of two adult sons who are now married and fathers themselves. I was fortunate to have been raised by a father in the home who took an active part in raising us seven children.

I would be remiss if I did not mention the many individuals I have worked and interacted with who are involved in the fatherhood movement, including direct-services providers and directors of fatherhood programs, both locally and nationally. I have also been inspired by many individuals who represented funding agencies locally, statewide, and at the federal level. They have been very passionate about the important roles that fathers play in the lives and the development of their children, family, community, and country.

1

The Fatherless Crisis

It has been well-documented that a father's presence matters in the family, community and, most importantly, with his children. A father's presence matters not just in terms of economic well-being, but also in terms of social support and child development. Many studies have shown that there is a link between a father's absence and a host of problems: juvenile delinquency, drug and alcohol abuse, violent crimes, promiscuity, teenage pregnancy, failure in school, mental health challenges, difficulty establishing friendships as children, and failed relationships later in life. These studies further show that children who grew up with fathers were happier, excelled in school skills, and had better problem-solving skills. They were also more likely to succeed as adults, both in their personal lives and in the workforce. Writers like Erick Brenner, Wade Horn, David Blankenhorn, James Levin, and Ed Pitt, have contributed to studies and pertinent information concerning the importance of father involvement in the lives of their children.

Today, there are a significant number of children who are growing up without a father or a significant male figure in their homes. Father absence continues to be a deep-rooted concern for families, communities, and society at large. This absence has a major negative impact on children, families, and communities. Although there has been an increase in programs across the country that focus on promoting responsible fatherhood, there continues to be a need to significantly expand and enhance these efforts. Of all of the programs across the nation that have focused on fatherhood development, some of the most noted successful programs include Charles Ballard's Institute for Responsible Fatherhood, Dads Make A Difference in Minnesota and the Young Fathers and Responsible Fathers Program in the State of Maryland.

The Clinton Administration focused on issues related to fathers and made attempts to have fathers involved in the lives of their children and in programs for children and families. In June 1995, an Executive Order was issued from President Clinton to the Heads of all Executive departments and agencies. This Order directed them to review every program, policy, and initiative that pertains to families to ensure they seek to engage and meaningfully include fathers. The Order also required agencies to modify their programs to include fathers and strengthen their involvement with their children.

The major social problems that are occurring in our communities today are closely related to "fatherlessness," and the fact that some fathers do not know how to be an effective father because they did not have an effective father role model while growing up. Addressing the needs of fathers will ultimately assist fathers in meeting the needs of their families, especially their children. I acknowledge that a number of fathers are fulfilling their financial, moral, and social responsibilities to their children and families; however, there continues to be a need to identify and eliminate barriers that prevent other fathers from fulfilling their God-ordained responsibility of fatherhood. I also acknowledge that a number of young and not-so-young fathers, who are faced with the many responsibilities of fatherhood, lack the needed skills to handle the responsibilities of fatherhood.

Although many states across this nation have developed effective programs to address the needs of this frequently underserved population, it is generally acknowledged that there continues to be a desperate need to help fathers understand the significant roles they play in the lives of their children. It is also recognized that fathers need to be equipped with the necessary skills and resources to enable them to become, or continue to be, responsible and accountable fathers. This is a desperate time for men to step up to the plate and become the most responsible fathers they can be for the benefit of their children, families and this nation.

Studies like William Doherty, Edward Kouneski and Maratha Erickson, ; David Blankenhorn, and Vivian Gadsden , noted the impact of father absent homes on children. Also three out of four teenage suicides occur in households where a parent has been absent, and 90% of homeless and runaway children are from fatherless homes. It is well-documented that fatherlessness is currently the most significant family and social problem facing America, as well as other countries. This crisis is also having a devastating impact on the African-American community. If something is not implemented immediately, we are headed for continued destruction of the African-American community and possibly a culture.

This National Fatherhood Institute Fact sheet is instructive:

Top Ten Father Facts

- 24 million children (34 percent) live absent of their biological fathers.
- Nearly 20 million children (27 percent) live in single-parent homes.
- 1.35 million births (33 percent of all births) in 2000 occurred out of wedlock.
- 43 percent of first marriages dissolve within fifteen years; about 60 percent of divorcing couples have children; and approximately one million children each year experience the divorce of their parents.
- Over 3.3 million children live with an unmarried parent and the parent's cohabiting partner. The number of cohabiting couples with children has nearly doubled since 1990, from 891,000 to 1.7 million today.
- Fathers who live with their children are more likely to have a close, enduring relationship with their children than those who do not. The best predictor of father presence is marital status. Compared to children born within marriage, children born to cohabiting parents are three times as likely to experience father absence, and children born to unmarried, non-cohabiting parents are four times as likely to live in a father-absent home.
- About 40 percent of children in father-absent homes have not seen their father at all during the past year; 26 percent of absent fathers live in a different state than their children; and 50 percent of children living absent of their father have never set foot in their father's home.
- Children who live absent of their biological fathers are, on average, at least two to three times more likely to be poor; to use drugs; to experience educational, health, emotional and behavioral problems; to be victims of child abuse; and to engage in criminal behavior than their peers who live with their married, biological (or adoptive) parents.
- From 1960 to 1995, the proportion of children living in single-parent homes tripled, from 9 percent to 27 percent, and the proportion of children living with married parents declined; however, from 1995 to 2000, the proportion of children living in single-parent homes slightly declined, while the proportion of children living with two married parents remained stable.
- Children with involved, loving fathers are significantly more likely to do well in school, have healthy self-esteem, exhibit empathy and pro-social behavior, and avoid high-risk behaviors like drug use, truancy, and criminal activity compared to children who have uninvolved fathers.

I do not want to downplay or negate the major contributions and significant impact single mothers have had on the successful rearing of children without a positive male's involvement. Single mothers are responsible for rearing many of our nation's most successful men and fathers. This is not an attack on single mothers, but an emergency call for men to fulfill their inherent roles and responsibilities as effective men and fathers. Any program that provides services to men must incorporate a component of their outreach services to the mother and other family members. We must treat the family holistically and not isolate any one member for intervention.

2

Understanding Your Responsibilities as a Man and Father

There is a desperate need for fathers to understand their role and responsibilities as a man and a father. Some of these roles include that of a leader, provider, nurturer, teacher, priest of the home, visionary, goal setter, disciplinarian, caregiver, guide, and, most importantly, one who provides unconditional love. Fathers also need to provide to their children, both boys and girls, with examples of what it means to be a good, respectable, and responsible man.

The Father's Role from a Biblical Perspective

The biblical role of the husband and a father can, at first, appear overwhelming and impossible to achieve; however, we should take courage because God has prepared men, genetically and spiritually, to fulfill these roles and responsibilities. As noted in His Word, God never commands us to do something that He has not equipped us to do.

Man as a Leader: God has made it very clear in His Word that the man should be the leader of his home, just as God is the head of the Church. It is the father's responsibility to understand his role and responsibilities from a biblical perspective. This can be done by searching the Scriptures to obtain wisdom and understanding of God's instructions for a man and father. We should be aware that God created us to have a relationship with Him and part of our responsibility is to study His Word, be obedient to His Word, fellowship with other believers, and, most importantly, worship God. We need to think of ourselves as God's representatives on Earth, because some people will only get to know what God is like through us. We should be aware that a man, especially a father, needs to live a life that displays the characteristics of God. These characteristics include the fruit of the spirit as noted in Galatians 5:22-23 (love, joy, peace, longsuffering, gentleness, goodness, faith, meekness, temperance).

Because we are made in the image of God, we need to display characteristics like kindness, consideration of others, and love for one another, especially our enemies. As the Bible states in 1st Corinthians 13, (Love is patient and kind; not jealous or conceited or proud. Love is not ill mannered, or selfish or irritable. Love does not keep a record of wrongs and, finally, love is not happy with evil).

A man needs to be the motivator for his family, especially his children. He must motivate them to set goals, complete tasks, be obedient, and take responsibility for their behavior and other responsibilities. A man must also remember that he was created with the God-given ability to lead. Genesis 1:26 states, "And God said, 'Let us make a man in our image, according to our likeness, and let him have dominion over the fish of the sea, over the fowl of the air and over the cattle, over all the earth and over every creeping thing that creeps on the earth."

The father should take a leadership role in his family. He should create goals and visions for himself and his family. This includes short-term and long-term goals. The family should be involved in creating these goals and visions, but the father should take the leadership role in this process, always seeking guidance from God. This will require daily communication with God and reading Scripture.

A man should ask himself, "Where do I see my family and myself in three, five, or ten years from now?" It is important to have personal and family goals that include, but are not limited to, the following categories:

- **SPIRITUAL**
- **INDIVIDUAL**
- **FAMILY**
- **EMPLOYMENT (INCLUDING OWNING YOUR OWN BUSINESS)**

- **FINANCIAL**
- **PHYSICAL**
- **PERSONAL**
- **RELAX TIME**

Man as a Teacher: The father needs to take the leadership role in teaching his children about God; that includes the plan of salvation, the importance of church, and both attendance and active participation in various ministries within the church. It is vitally important for the father to take his rightful role within the family to train his children the way they should go, as noted in Proverbs 22:6. In *The Message*, (The Bible in Contemporary Language by Eugene H. Peterson) this passage states, "Point your kids in the right direction—when they're old they won't be lost."

As a father, you should help your children know the joy of obedience and the value of character. Genesis 18:19 states, "I have chosen him to teach his family to obey Me forever and to do what is right and fair. Then I will give Abraham many descendants just as I promised." A father is also responsible for the discipline of his children. He should be a wise counselor who leads his children in righteousness. "Fathers don't exasperate your children by coming down hard on them. Take them by the hand and lead them in the way of the Master" (Ephesians 6:4 *The Message*).

Father as a Provider: The man is responsible for providing for the needs of his family. According to 1 Timothy 5:8, "If anyone does not provide for his relatives, especially his immediate family, he has denied his faith and is worse than an unbeliever." 2 Thessalonians 3:10 notes, "We also gave you the rule that if you don't work you don't eat." Fathers need to have high work ethics and be a responsible man and meet the needs of his family financially, emotionally and spiritually.

Father as the Protector: The father is the protector of his family, both physically and spiritually. He is the guardian of his family, and he is responsible for defending them from criticism and to protect them from evil influences and the dangers of youthful desires. He should also take an active role in the courtship and dating of his children. He should pray for his children daily and pray with them before they go to school, during the day, and at night when they are in bed. Especially during the day, while the father is at work, he should pause to pray for his children and the entire family.

While attending a Promise Keepers Conference titled "Unleashed" in Baltimore, Maryland, in June 2006, one of the speakers, Samuel Rodriguez, noted that his father prayed for him daily during his school years and does the same for his children. The prayer included the following:

- That God would protect his children from evil
- That God would protect them with the blood of Jesus
- His children would fulfill their purpose in life

Father as the Priest: Fathers need to be aware that God has ordained men to be the priests of their homes. Fathers should begin or continue to have Bible study in the home on a regular basis. It is also important to lead your family in prayer in your home on a daily basis. This should include information that was presented by your Pastor or the Pastor who presented the Word during service, and continue to have further discussions on the message given. Fathers should have some discussion about what each of their family members received from the message, and suggestions for further study and implementation of the message in your daily lives. The children need to see their father actively reading the Bible and praying.

Dr. George Matthews II of Birmingham, AL noted in his discussion of "Men/Fathers From Issachar" (based on 1 Chronicles 12:32-40) that when a father is in his appropriate God-ordained place in his family, it produces a sense of joy and security in everything in which he is involved. A man/father should represent a reward or payment and refreshment in his children's and family's life. He should represent a blessing in the lives of his children and wife/mother of his children. He further noted that a man is anointed to lift others up, to advance and to move things along. He is also anointed to face challenges in a positive way; he is a producer of new ideas and concepts. A father has the ability to take things to the next level, and much more. He helps to make relationships easy. He is also a helper, and does not mind doing whatever is necessary to make the house function better, including domestic tasks. A father is anointed to handle challenges effectively and does not buckle under pressure. He has the stamina and is capable of forward thinking to protect his family and be an encouragement to all family members as well as other relatives and friends.

An effective father also teaches his children respect, and he displays respect for his wife and other women and does not go around making negative comments about his wife or women in general. An Issachar man is supposed to be a token of how much God loves the people by placing the father into their lives (children, their mother, and so forth). As fathers, we should be aware that we are supposed to be a reflection of how much God loves people, our wives and our children, and we should ask ourselves if we present the type of behavior, attitude, leadership, love, and support towards our family that represents the unconditional love of God????

Another important concept noted by Minister Matthews was that the father is supposed to be the builder of the family name. Questions we need to ask ourselves as fathers include the following:

- What kind of reputation or family name are you building for your family?
- What kind of name are you going to build and leave as a legacy?
- What kind of father will your children say you were after you have passed?
- What kind of father/husband will your wife/significant other say you were?
- How would your friends, co-workers, neighbors, and others describe you as a man/father?

These are some of the questions men need to ask themselves, and if there are areas of their lives that needs to be changed, they should do it now!!! Men need to leave a positive legacy for their children and others to build on and benefit from.

Fathers as a Role Model

It is extremely important for fathers to realize that they play an important function as a role model for their children. Fathers need to develop the necessary skills to be a positive role model for their children. Fathers need to realize their children are always watching them. They observe everything you do to see if you are gentle or angry towards them and others; whether or not you lie or tell the truth, and if you are supportive or always critical and judgmental. They know if you get high (use illegal drugs) or not, talk problems out in a calm manner or refuse to talk (shut down), and so forth. They also observe how you treat others, especially your wife or significant other, friends, relatives, co-workers, and neighbors. Always remember your children learn from the things you do and the choices you make. It is important that fathers demonstrate positive traits so their children can develop into productive, honest individuals with high moral standards.

The National Fatherhood Initiative also noted that fathers are role models to their children whether they realize it or not. A girl who spends time with a loving and supporting father grows up knowing she deserves to be treated with respect by boys and what to look for in a husband. Fathers have an opportunity to teach sons what is important in life by demonstrating honesty, humility, and responsibility. It is also important that fathers create an emotionally supportive environment for everyone in the home. By creating a culture of appreciation in your home, family members can feel it is a safe place where everyone can be free to express their thoughts and fears.

In summary, the late Larry Burkett noted in an article in the *Manna* (Good News For Delmarva) titled "Our Fathers – Our Examples," the Word of God is very explicit on what God expects from fathers. God expects fathers to be:

- Head of their households (Ephesians 5:23).
- Wise counselors who lead their children in righteousness (Genesis 18:19; Ephesians 6:1-3).
- Strong, reliable and confident (Psalms 103:13; Matthew 7:12).
- Good providers (2 Thessalonians 3:10).
- Sure to make time for those they love and to pray for their children daily (Proverbs 22:6).

Roles and Responsibilities of a Husband from a Biblical Perspective

Husbands have an awesome responsibility as the leader of the home and a biblically-based marriage. The blueprint for a marriage is noted in God's Word and represents the relationship between Jesus Christ and the church. As noted in Ephesians 5:23, a husband is the head of his wife as Christ is head of the Church. A husband is also required to love his wife like Christ loves the church. This love is unconditional or agape love, and is not based on how the husband is treated by the wife. He is to love his wife as himself. His goal should be to have oneness in a marriage relationship and to be more interested in serving his wife than his wife serving him.

A husband should strive to be transparent with his wife where he can share all of his concerns, fears, struggles, and more, without feeling that she will use this self-disclosure against him. As stated in 1 Corinthians 13:4-8 "Love is kind and patient, never jealous, boastful, proud, or rude. Love isn't selfish or quick-tempered. It doesn't keep a record of wrongs that others do. Love rejoices in the truth, but not in evil. Love is always supportive, loyal, hopeful and trusting. Love never fails!" With Christ as our example, a husband is required to treat his wife with love and kindness. He is required to be humble, supportive, sympathetic, and compassionate towards her.

Whenever there is disagreement between a husband and wife, he should not use inappropriate language towards her, no put-downs, no threatening remarks; he should use positive, non-verbal communication. He should avoid such non-verbal communications as frowns, pointing fingers, waiving arms, or any other gestures that will indicate negative communication.

Remember, in order to honor God in your marriages, you need to provide servant-leadership and to always love your wife as Christ loves the church.

What Happens When Dad Is Not There

The negative impact of absent-father homes can be lasting and serious. Without an active and involved father in the home, his children are more likely to be involved in drugs, experience failure in school, become involved in the criminal justice system, engage in sex at an earlier age, face an increased risk of having a child out of wedlock, and experience more mental health problems, and more. Father absence is not the only cause of these challenges, but it is a major influence.

From working in the field of human services, I have come in contact with children from ages seven to young adults, and adults who have experienced the impact of an absent father. Most all of them suffer from abandonment issues including, but not limited to, lack of self-esteem, anger management, poor relationships with men, and lack of trust. Nationally, we are finally getting a better understanding of what happens to a child when the biological father is not active in their life. This issue has drawn national attention and has had a positive impact on policies and programs that impact fathers, families and children.

Impact of Fatherlessness on Our Communities

The impact of fatherlessness on our country and especially on the African-American community is devastating. Some statistical data from the National Practitioners Network for Fathers and Families, Inc. includes the following:

- 63% of youth suicides are from fatherless homes.
- 85% of all children who exhibit behavioral disorders come from fatherless homes.
- 71% of all high school dropouts come from fatherless homes.
- A survey of over 20,000 parents found that when fathers are more involved in their children's education, including attending

school meetings and volunteering at school, children are more likely to get A's, enjoy school, participate in extracurricular activities and less likely to have repeated a grade.

- Young children living with unmarried mothers were five times as likely to be poor and ten times more likely to be extremely poor.
- Children who live with one parent have lower grade point averages, lower college aspirations, poorer attendance records, and higher dropout rates than students who live with both parents.
- Children who live with their single mothers are more likely to develop disruptive and anxiety disorders than children who live with both parents.
- Daughters of divorced or separated parents evidenced significantly higher rates of internalizing problems, like anxiety and depression.
- Children from single-mother families have less of an ability to delay gratification and poorer impulse control, like control over anger and sexual gratification.

Other statistical information about father absence includes a 1999 Princeton University study, "Father Absence and Youth Incarceration," which observed that "as the incidence of father absence grows, community disintegration and crime, especially youth crime, will continue to grow." This study also noted that father absence is linked to the following additional statistics:

- 90% of all homeless and run away youth
- 70% of youths in state institutions
- 75% of adolescent patients in substance abuse centers
- 80% of rapists who are motivated by displaced anger

The Child Welfare League of America noted that children who have been abused and neglected are 67 times more likely than other children to be arrested between ages 9 and 12. These children typically are found in fatherless homes in which boyfriends and stepfathers often view them as nuisances. Fathers accounted for 93% of incarcerated parents. It should also be noted that fathers in the United States spend less time with their children than fathers in any other country. Research shows that among those fathers who do live with their children, the average amount of time spent with them is twelve (12) minutes a day. This practice is unacceptable and fathers need to be educated or re-educated on the importance of spending quality time with their children.

3

Contributions Fathers Make in the Lives of Their Children

Fathers need to have a good understanding of the contributions they make in the lives of their children. An available, involved, and responsible father's contribution to the growth and healthy development of their children is immeasurable. It has been well documented that young children with involved fathers possess the following skills:

- Greater empathy
- Enhanced social skills
- Less gender role stereotyping
- More awareness of needs and rights of others
- More generousity
- More compassion towards others
- Higher self-esteem
- More self-control and less impulsive
- More emotionally intelligence
- More independence
- More confidence with exploration
- More ambition
- Less susceptible to peer pressure
- More competency
- More liked and acceptable by other children
- More self-reliance
- More self-confident with males and females

Children who grow up with an involved father display the following characteristics:

- Increased curiosity
- Increased exploration of the world around them
- Less hesitance and fear in new situations
- Greater tolerance for stress and frustrations
- More willingness to try new things.

In the area of cognitive development of children, father involvement has the following benefits:

- Higher verbal skills
- Higher scores on assessment of cognitive competence
- Increased competence in math
- Son's IQ level is significantly related to father's nurturing

16 Skill Sets for Father Involvement

It is extremely important that we fathers continue to be actively involved with our children. Here are the 16 skill steps that have been identified as essential for that involvement:

1. Assist boys in controlling aggression
2. Teach boys about male responsibility
3. Assist boys in displaying more social confidence
4. Help children adapt to change more easily
5. Have increased empathy for others
6. Have a close and warm relationship with our daughters so we produce girls with a sense of competence
7. Assist girls in understanding what a meaningful and respectful relationship should be with a man
8. Contribute to the child's ability to take initiative and evidence of self-control through father involvement
9. Teach boys how to be men and teach girls to expect respect from men
10. Be our daughters' first date and set the example of a real, responsible man
11. Provide guidance and discipline
12. Help boys define their masculinity
13. Assist children in developing appropriate socialization skills
14. Develop respect for adults

15. Assist our children in knowing how to recognize and appropriately deal with highly charged emotions
16. Help stimulate intellectual development

Father involvement has many other important contributions in child development, like a nurturer. Appropriate nurturing assists in the emotional development of the child. The importance of father-child play activities that assist in building trusting and supportive relationships is extremely important in the development of the child. By participating in this type of activity, we as fathers build a positive connection with our children. We should also use every opportunity when the child is young to feed, bathe, and participate in other activities that assist in connecting with the child in a positive way. Mothers should encourage and support positive father/child interaction.

John Rosemond also noted the unique and crucial role fathers play in the lives of their children. He also recognized that it is not enough just to be present in the home. Fathers must be actively involved and a vigorously interested participant in the child-rearing process. Rosemond offers six ways to become more involved with your child:

1   Find an activity you and your child can do together and make time for it regularly.
2. Help (but not force) your child to develop hobbies and interests.
3. As your child grows through the teen years, become less a disciplinarian and more a mentor.
4. Talk to your child and keep communication lines open by being a good listener.
5. Love your child's mother with all your heart.
6. Remember a child is never too old to be told "I love you."

Daughters need their Fathers

The impact of a father's absence in their daughters lives can be devastating. Frequently, these girls will grow up experiencing issues of abandonment, rejection, depression, loneliness, anxiety, and other emotional pain. She may revert to filling the void in her life with substance abuse, eating disorders (like anorexia and bolemia), suicide, sexual activity with several men, same sex involvement, and so forth. As teenagers and adults, these women may have a difficult time establishing a positive relationship with men. Frequently, these women will spend most of their lives searching for the love, affection, and nurturing that they did not receive from their biological father. Because of the high potential of these negative effects on women, it is extremely important that fathers have a positive, nurturing, and supportive relationship with their daughters regardless of the relationship between them and the mothers of the children. When the father provides the daughter with the proper support, affirmation, and nurturing, she is more likely not to accept negative behavior from a man who does not demonstrate a respectful, loving, and supporting relationship.

Dad and Daughters, a non-profit organization in Duluth, MN, offers these excellent tips for dads with daughters:

10 Tips for Dads with Daughters

1. Listen to girls. Focus on what is really important—what my daughter thinks, believes, feels, dreams, and does—rather than how she looks.
2. Encourage her strength and celebrate her savvy. Help my daughter learn to recognize, resist and overcome barriers. Help her develop her strengths to achieve her goals. Help her be what Girls Incorporated calls Strong, Smart and Bold!!!
3. Respect her uniqueness. Urge her to love her body and discourage

dieting. Make sure your daughter knows that you love her for who she is and see her as a whole person, capable of anything. Remember your daughter is likely to choose a life partner who acts like you and has your values. So, treat her and those she loves with respect. Remember the following:

- Growing girls need to eat often and healthy;
- Dieting increases the risk of eating disorders (and usually doesn't work); and
- She has her body for what it can do, not how it looks.

Advertisers spend billions to convince my daughter she doesn't look "right." I won't buy into it.

4. Get physically active with your daughter. Play catch, tag, jump rope, basketball, frisbee, hockey, soccer, or just take walks…you name it!! Help her learn all the great things her body can do. Physically active girls are less likely to get pregnant, drop out of school, or put up with an abusive partner. Studies show that the most physically active girls have <u>fathers</u> who are active with them. Being physically active with her is a great investment!!!

5. Get involved in your daughter's school. Volunteer, chaperone, and read to her class. Ask tough questions, like: Does the school have and use an eating disorder prevention or body image awareness program? Does it tolerate sexual harassment from boys or girls? Do more boys take advanced math and science classes and if so, why? Are at least half the student leaders girls?

6. Get involved in your daughter's activities. Volunteer to drive, coach, assist with a play, assist in teaching a class—anything!! Demand equality.

7. Help make the world better for girls. This world holds dangers for daughters. Work with other parents to demand an end to violence against females, media sexualization of girls, pornography, and advertisers making billions feeding on daughters' insecurities and all "boys are more important than girls" attitudes.

8. Take your daughter to work with you. Participate in every official Take You Daughters to Work campaign and make sure your place of employment participate. Show her who pays your bills and manages your finances. Our daughters will have a job some day, so you need to introduce them to the world of work and finances!!

9. Support positive alternative media for girls. Join with your family to watch programs that portray smart, savvy girls. Subscribe to healthy girl-edited magazines. It's not enough to condemn what's bad, you must support and use media that support daughters.

10. Talk to other fathers. Together, we fathers have many years of experience and encouragement to share. There is much we can learn from each other. We can also have a significant positive influence and make the world better for girls when we work together.

I highly recommend a book by Jonetta Rose Barras, titled *Whatever Happened to Daddy's Little Girl?* This is an excellent description about the impact that being fatherless has on women, and the author's personal experience as a woman who grew up without the presence of her biological father. She shares her personal struggles about this issue and offers a detailed description of the "Fatherless Woman Syndrome." Again, this book is a must-read to better understand the relationship between fathers and daughters and what happens when dad is not there.

5

Single Fathers

A great deal of emphasis and resources are available for married couples and single mothers. Unfortunately, there is limited information and assistance available for single fathers, although there has been an increase in homes where single fathers are raising their children. Writer Doug Carroll (2003) offers a thoughtful set of tips for single fathers challenged with raising their children:

1. **Put your children first.** This is your living legacy we're talking about. Jobs come and go, but this is the most important work you will ever do.
2. **Be unstoppable as a father.** You can be as good as you want to be. Don't make excuses for why you can't.
3. **Get over your anger, hurt, and guilt—and get on with being a dad.** Your children need you too much. The will to stay connected with them needs to be stronger than your feelings of pain.
4. **Financial child support is the beginning of responsibility, not the end of it.**
5. **Quantity time and quality time are more similar than you think.**
6. **Listen, ask, and share.** You won't have a child's respect without a relationship. Be fully present.
7. **Model, don't lecture.** Show, don't tell.
8. **Keep investing in your children, even when there is no visible return.**
9. **Bathe everything you do in love.**
10. **Remember that no one but you can be Dad.** It has been noted that most American children suffer from too much mother and too little father.

For those fathers who spend an enormous amount of time at work and even work while at home in the evenings and weekends as well as on vacations, author Robert Blodgett offers these six steps to assist fathers in prioritizing their family in a workaholic world:

1. **Make a written commitment to your family.** Develop a short, one-page contract that spells out actions you'll take to ensure your family is a top priority. Write down how you intend to balance your work duties with your family duties. Then, sign the contract and display it prominently in your home.

2. **Make career decisions with your family.** As you contemplate job moves, promotions or transfers, discuss it together as a family. Make sure you explain the fine details of the job, including the hours you'll work, the travel required and the overtime that might be included. And then, make the decision as a family whether or not the job is worth taking.

3. **Avoid work during family prime time.** Carve out a time each day that your work will not intrude. Turn off the mobile phone, close down the laptop, let the machine answer the phone, and take that time to be completely focused on your family. Dinnertime is a good time for doing this.

4. **Communicate your performance on the job.** When at work, create a status report that lists your assignments, their status and any pending issues or questions. This allows your boss to evaluate you on performance rather than other measurements, like time in the office. It helps to demonstrate that even though you have a family-first commitment, you are a critical contributor to the organization.

5. **Involve your co-workers in your commitment.** Your co-workers, and even your boss, can be terrific support mechanism for your loyalty to family. Make your commitment known and ask them to respect and support it. Be ready to do the same thing for them.

6. **Don't work on weekends or vacations.** This is a time to give you and your family a chance to decompress. But that can't happen if your work habitually intrudes. Take a stand that when you venture off on vacation, you won't allow work to intrude. If that's not possible, then reschedule your vacation to another time. For weekends, don't fall into the habit of committing yourself to

work. While sometimes you may need that extra time for special projects, be careful not to let those special times turn into a regular habit.

The Need for Accountable and Responsible Men in All of Our Communities

I realize we have many men in our families and community who are aware of their roles and responsibilities, and are fulfilling them. I commend those men, and I hope the information in this book will help them to enhance their efforts at being effective, available and responsible fathers. It is long overdue that we begin to make the men in our community accountable and responsible for their children, if they do not take that responsibility. We must not tolerate this type of irresponsible behavior from men within our families and community. We must educate them about their roles and responsibilities as fathers; the impact they play on the growth and healthy development of their children; and the importance of them being actively involved with their children. Again, I must emphasize that irresponsible fathers must not be tolerated in our families and communities. It is essential that men begin to make a commitment that they will not allow a child to be raised without the presence of their father even if the mother of the child and the father do not get along or are engaged in other relationships. The parents must agree on doing what is in the best interest of their child regardless of their relationship.

Men need to realize that they set the tone for self-esteem, cognitive development, spiritual development, stress and conflict resolution, self-control, and interpersonal relationships. We need to educate our men about the unique contributions they make to the lives of their children. We also need to combat the negative forces that are plaguing our communities by developing responsible and accountable men and fathers. We need to focus on leading by example and develop strategies to immediately address the fatherlessness crisis in the African-American community. It has been proved that we can no longer totally depend on the government to solve the problems in our community. We must begin to initiate our own interventions if our community and the current and future generations are going to survive.

Fathers and men need to surround themselves with positive people. If you are involved with men who are not going anywhere and are not trying to have a positive relationship with their children and the mother of their children, you need to distance yourself from them, even if they are relatives.

Accountability

It would also be beneficial if men would develop a relationship with one or a few positive men to whom they could be accountable. They should have contact with this individual(s) on a regular basis, preferably weekly, so they could monitor the behavior in areas they are struggling with. These areas could include substance abuse, infidelity, spending quality time with their children and their wives and significant others, managing finances, praying for and with their families, and so forth. Men should be honest with their support group when addressing the status of their behavior by addressing some of the challenges they are dealing with.

6

Healing Your Father Wounds

The Need to Develop Knowledge and Understanding of the Impact of Your Father Wound

It is extremely important that both men and fathers develop knowledge and understanding of the impact of the "father wound." The father wound is the result of those negative experiences we all had with our fathers, whether they were present or absent (physically or emotionally). We need to understand the areas where we feel our fathers were inadequate or just did not meet our physical or emotional needs for whatever reason. All of these experiences have an impact on our lives, and it is necessary that we examine and try to understand its impact on us today. This requires us to concentrate and go back to visualize and mentally experience our relationships with our fathers or father figures in our lives.

We need to determine if they were supportive fathers and always there when we needed them or if they were abusive (both physically, emotionally and sexually), critical, judgmental, absent, present physically but absent emotionally, and more.

Some fathers were judgmental, frequently critical, and controlling. We had difficulty obtaining their approval of the things we did. Sometimes these dads would compare us to our other siblings or other children they knew.

Some dads were distant and preoccupied with work or other activities in the home or just did not communicate frequently with their children. They were not involved in the children's education or hobbies. Going back and remembering those relationships may be emotionally difficult for some, but it is a mandatory exercise for emotional healing. Being raised by an abusive, critical father can result in our having to endure deep, emotional pain inside. Some of the possible consequences of an ineffective father-child relationship that can impact us as adults could possibly include the following:

- Mistrust
- Anxiety
- Abandonment
- Bitterness and anger
- Fear of rejection
- Unhealthily relationships with men and women
- Depression
- Self-critical and guilt-ridden
- Fear of success
- Defensiveness
- Unrealistic expectation about what men are like
- Feelings of dependency
- Insufficient self-discipline
- Prone to stay in unhealthy relationships
- A need to be in control
- A great need to receive attention from others
- Unrealistic need for approval
- Prone to psychosomatic illnesses like headaches, high blood pressure, ulcers, strokes, and other stress-related illnesses.

Frequently, individuals will function as adults with an empty space inside of them that longs to be filled by their biological father. Our Heavenly Father can meet all of our needs, including feelings we experience as a result of living in an absent or inadequate father environment.

Nevertheless, there is still the yearning of a child to know his or her biological father. There is also a need to heal from past experiences with your biological father by probing and reconnecting with the past. Some of the things you can do to adequately address your father loss include the following:

- Write a letter to your father regardless if he is living or deceased and express your true feelings to include your hurts, fears, disappointments, wishes or confusion.
- Arrange to have a face-to-face conversation with your father, if living, and be honest about all of the feelings you experienced as a child and as an adult, based on your relationship or lack of one with him.
- Role play by sitting in a chair and talking to an empty chair visualizing talking to your father in an open and honest manner.

Whatever you do, you need to address the issues of your childhood experience, put forth an effort to say good-by to the father of your youth and to get on with your life as effectively as possible.

The Importance of Forgiveness

Forgiveness is essential to effective healing. You have to let go of the hurt, disappointments, and other pain that you experienced as a child in your relationship with your father. Your goal should be to give up your resentment towards him and release him and yourself from the mistakes of the past. This can be a very difficult process, but it must be done so you can live a peaceful life without harboring significant hatred and resentment towards your father or others in your life. Some recommendations to address this issue are to do the following:

- Forget trying to get your dad and others to understand how much they hurt you. The person who hurt you may never totally understand how much they hurt you.
- Forgiveness unblocks your energy and you can move on to a healthier and more fulfilling way of existing.
- If you don't forgive, it can develop into psychosomatic illnesses, like heart problems, cancer, strokes, high blood pressure, headaches, ulcers, chest pains, and so forth.

As noted by Ray Pritchard in his book on forgiveness, forgiveness is not about you or the person who hurt you. Instead, it is all about God. God's commandment is for us to forgive those who trespass against us. If we want God to forgive us for our sins, we need to forgive others. This is a hard lesson to learn, but it is necessary so you can release not only yourself but also the one who hurt you. It is extremely important that you honestly acknowledge your feelings about how your father hurt you and did not provide the fathering experiences you needed. It is also important that you release those negative feelings you have about your father. Your father probably only gave you what was available or what he knew to give based upon his experiences with his own father. We have to focus on the positives of our fathers and stop spending time on their negative characteristics. We have to refocus and bury those past experiences and put our energies on the present and future. As men, we should make sure we do not repeat the past mistakes of our fathers and focus on being the best dads we can be for our children, families, communities, and our nation.

7

Making Time to be a Father

Fathers and Their Children

As noted earlier, fathers play a major role in the development of their children, and they need to put forth the effort to make their children physically, emotionally, and spiritually healthy. The following are some important recommendations from various sources to assist fathers in meeting the overall needs of their children:

10 Ways to Make Time for Your Children

The National Fatherhood Initiative noted the following 10 ways a father can make time for his children:

1. Commit to a family mealtime each day.
2. Write your children's activities into your schedule.
3. Identify one thing on your weekly schedule you can do without and replace it with kid time.
4. Take one of your children along when you run errands.
5. Volunteer to participate in a regularly scheduled child activity, like coaching a baseball or football team or helping with a school activity.
6. Identify one children's show on TV that you secretly like to watch and make a point of watching it with your child.
7. Develop an interest in a hobby you and your child can enjoy together.
8. If your work requires that you travel and your business trip can be extended into a long weekend, take one of your children along with you.

9.   If your work schedule is flexible, start your work day earlier so you can get home earlier in the afternoon to be with your family.

10.   Leave your work, cellular phones, and pagers at home when you go on family vacations and outings.

The National Practitioners Network for Fathers and Families also produced a brochure, made possible through a grant from the General Mills Foundation, that noted the following fifteen ways a father can support his child:

1.   **Show your children that you love them.** Hugs, kisses, encouraging words, pats on the back, spending time together are all ways to express your love.

2.   **Communicate with your child's mother.** Talk about what is happening with your child, discuss decisions to be made, and more. Remember that communication means talking and listening. Listening is a major part of communicating. Find time and ways that you can communicate with your child's mother so you both have the information you need.

3.   **Do your part to take care of your child's physical needs.** Share the daily activities of keeping you child fed, clothed, clean and happy.

4.   **Take care of your child's health.** Go on routine and sick doctor visits, be sure your child is immunized, know first aid, and childproof your home.

5.   **Take care of yourself.** You can't be there for your child if you are sick, a substance abuser, in jail or worse. Avoid drugs, alcohol, and tobacco. Carefully choose the people who visit your home. Avoid unsafe situations and stay away from guns.

6.   **Encourage your child's development by providing appropriate playtime, guidance, and encouragement.** Learn about child development so you will know what to expect and can be prepared for the many ways your child will learn and grow.

7.   **Take care of your child financially.** Accept responsibility through a declaration of paternity or other means. If you are responsible for paying child support, pay it on time. Improve yourself through education and training so you can get the job you need to support your child.

8.   **When necessary, discuss and work out custody and**

visitation. Cooperate and compromise when it is best for your child.

9. **Support your child's learning.** Help your child grow and learn through play. As your child gets older, be involved in their school, help with homework and projects, and volunteer. Children who have fathers who are interested and involved in their education do far better that those who don't.

10. **Keep your child safe when he/she is with you.** Be sure your home and anywhere you visit are childproof. Use a properly installed car seat in all vehicles. Never leave your child alone at home, on a playground, in a car, or near water. Protect your child at all times.

11. **Shared parenting means sharing the responsibility and decisions of raising your child with the other parent.** This can be challenging, whether or not the parents live together. Your goal should be to make shared parenting work.

12. **Spend time with your child.** Your father-child time is special so focus on your child. Do not plan on watching t.v., playing your favorite video game, or hanging out with friends. You must spend quality time with your child on a regular basis.

13. **Family schedules should work for you, the mother and especially your child.** Try to accommodate your child's naptime, meal times, and other routines in daily activities. Keep this in mind if you schedule visitation, too.

14. **Be patient.** Kids get tired, sick, whiny, irritable, and make messes. Dealing with it is part of being a dad.

15. **Remember that you are always a dad.** What you do—or don't do—for your child will make a difference. Do the right thing and be there to love, support and guide your child.

The National Center for Fathers in Kansas City, MO (ncf@aol.com) noted that children hunger for father involvement. The future is in the hands of fathers. Fathers have the power to shape generations. The organization noted the following five things fathers can do to shape the future:

1. **Express affection and listen actively:**

- Do you tell your child "good job" when they complete a task?
- Do you show affection to your children?

- Do you touch or hug your child in appropriate ways? (Physical affection is important, particularly for daughters.)
- Do you actively listen to your children?

Expressing affection also involves learning to listen. Some recommendations to become a more effective active listener are as follows:

- Make eye contact. Get on the same level with your child. This will open the door for a heart-to-heart talk.
- Ask questions or paraphrase back your child's words. This helps you make sure you understand what your child is saying.
- Nod or signal physically that you are listening.
- Stay relaxed.
- Physically put away or turn off any distractions like the newspapers or television. Avoid taking telephone calls or other interruptions during these discussions.

2.   Be involved in your children's education.

You can be involved or more involved in your children's education by doing the following:

- Identify your child's learning style: talking and listening; touching and doing; or watching. This will help them and their teachers.
- Take your children to the library and let them browse and show you what they're interested in.
- Put an encouraging note in the textbook of your child's hardest subject.
- Teach your children things, like how to check and add oil to the car.
- Expose your children to other cultures by inviting ethnic and international friends to your home.

3.   Be consistent.

Imagine the type of compass used to draw circles on paper. As a father, you are the pivot point that remains steady in the center. Be that point of reference for your child by being predictable:

- In your daily schedule
- In your moods
- In your activities
- In your ethics
- In keeping your promises

4.   Work on being aware of your children and their world.

Your child's world changes and your child changes. The following are seven ideas for increasing your awareness:

- Ask your children who their all-time hero is.
- Go to a sports event at your child's school, even if your child isn't on the team.
- Check out a book from the library on the stages of a child's growth.
- Invite one of your child's friends over for a meal.
- Ask your children what causes them the most stress.
- Call your child on the phone and ask what is the most difficult challenge facing him or her.
- Listen to your children's favorite piece of music and ask them about it.

5.   Commit your life. Invest your time.

Children spell love, T-I-M-E. Here's a chance to get some feedback on how you're doing as a father. Rate yourself (with 5 being very good, 4- good, 3 – average, 2 – fair, and 1 – poor) on how successful your are in these areas:

1. Spending a few minutes of additional time with each child every day._____
2. Eating the evening meal together as a family. _____
3. Putting time in my schedule to attend my children's activities. _____
4. Giving time to my children when they need me. _____
5. Sacrificing some of my activities to spend time with my children. _____
6. Scheduling time to spend with my children. _____

TOTAL: _____

These questions came from the Personal Fathering Profile, a comprehensive feedback profile given to fathers across the nation. You can add your score and plot the total on a scale below, which is based on the norm of a national study of 2,066 fathers:

FATHERING FEEDBACK

6	16	19	25	28	30
POOR	FAIR	AVERAGE	GOOD	VERY GOOD	

In considering your score on this profile, think about:

1. How much time did your father spend with you?
2. When's the best time to "spend time" with your children?
3. What's the biggest barrier to spending time with your kids?

South Carolina ETV noted the following ten tips for fathers:

1. **Be there.**
   Children want and need your physical presence, from infancy onward.
2. **Listen.**
   Being there means more than being present physically.
3. **Support your partner.**
   Work together on behalf of your child whether you are living together or not.
4. **Learn to disagree appropriately with your partner.**
   Disagreement is a normal part of parenthood. It is how you resolve those differences that matter.
5. **Get to know and be known to the people in your child's world.**
   Teachers, caregivers, doctors—all of them are an important part.
6. **Get to know and be known to your children's friends and their parents.**
   If you have concerns about who your child is hanging out with, be sure to discuss this with your child.
7. **Play with your children.**
   One of the best ways to learn about and develop a lasting connection with your children is to play with them—to enter their world.

8. **Teach by example.**
   Children follow what you do more than what you say.
9. **Discipline with love.**
   To discipline means to guide or bring out the best in your child and that is best done with love.
10. **Keep your sense of humor.**
    Nobody said fatherhood is easy. If you can survive fatherhood, you can survive anything.

During a pre-school graduation ceremony for one of my grandsons, Noah, at the Paquin School in Baltimore Maryland, the following poem was shared with the audience and every child presented a copy of this very powerful poem to their parent(s).

"Children Learn What They Live"

If children live with **criticism**, they learn to **condemn**.
If children live with **hostility**, they learn to **fight**.
If children live with **fear,** they learn to be **apprehensive.**
If children live with **pity**, they learn to **feel sorry for themselves.**
If children live with **ridicule**, they learn to feel **shy**.
If children live with **jealousy**, they learn to feel **envy**.
If children live with **shame**, they learn to feel **guilty**.
If children live with **encouragement**, they learn **confidence**.
If children live with **tolerance**, they learn **patience**.
If children live with **praise**, they learn **appreciation**.
If children live with **acceptance**, they learn to **love**.
If children live with **approval**, they learn to **like themselves**.
If children live with **recognition**, they learn it is **good to have a goal**.
If children live with **sharing**, they learn **generosity**.
If children live with **honesty**, they learn **truthfulness**.
If children live with **fairness**, they learn **justice**.
If children live with **kindness** and consideration, they learn **respect**.
If children live with **security**, they learn to **have faith** in themselves and in those about them.
If children live with **friendliness**, they learn **the world is a nice place in which to live.**

(Author unknown)

8

Maintaining a Positive Attitude

The Need for Fathers to Develop and Maintain a Positive Relationship With Their Children's Mother

It is extremely important that fathers establish and maintain a positive,and supportive relationship between themselves and the mothers of their children, regardless of if they are married or not. Even if they are not currently in a romantic relationship, having a positive relationship with the mother is extremely important and beneficial to the fathers, the mothers, and especially the children. Children need to see that their parents respect each other and that they get along without constant conflict that goes unresolved.

It is also important that the parents put forth an honest effort to create a positive and calm atmosphere in the home where the child can feel supported, loved, and not experience negative conflict on a regular basis between parents.

Effective Conflict Resolution and Problem Solving Strategies

Conflict is something that will always occur in any relationship. It is a natural part of any relationship and it can be very beneficial in strengthening a relationship if handled appropriately. The important thing is how you handle the conflict. The goal for every conflict situation should be to strive for a win-win solution so both parties will be overall satisfied with the decision agreed upon. It is extremely important that you realize that compromise is the key element to addressing and solving conflict. Usually, conflict situations can result in improved interpersonal communication as well as personal growth. Parents will experience conflict in their relationship whether they are married or not. This most important thing is to manage the conflict and use it as a tool to better understand each other's point of view. The following are some recommendations on how you can handle conflict in an appropriate manner:

- Each individual should be allowed and encouraged to express their feelings regarding the conflict. Each individual should also take turns talking about their feelings without any interruptions from the other party.
- You should be honest with your feelings, but express them in a calm and gentle manner without raising your voice; frowning your face; pointing your fingers at your partner; or displaying other non-verbal inappropriate messages. You must also avoid name-calling, cursing, negative and put-down statements.
- You and your partner need to decide and agree on when is the best time to discuss the conflict in a calm, non-threatening manner.
- Each individual should agree not to get defensive and display concern and understanding of the other person's point of view although different from yours. Your focus should be to concentrate and try to understand your partner's point of view before expressing yours.
- While sharing your feelings, focus on how you feel without blaming your partner. Avoid using "You" statements and always use "I" statements. Focus on saying, "I feel" (hurt, disappointed, fearful, upset, angry, rejected, controlled, ashamed, embarrassed, and so forth) and not on "You" did this or that. This approach will take some concentration and practice, but it is the best approach to use.
- It is also important to try to focus on the present conflict and not to bring up the past.
- The next step is to express what you need from the other person to resolve the conflict. After you hear your partner openly express their feelings and what is needed, both parties must be willing to compromise and agree on a solution to address the conflict.
- Both parties should strive for a win-win solution at all times.

Another way to view and address conflict in a relationship is to use the following Problem Solving Model:

1. Identify the problem from both people's perspectives.
2. Discuss and agree on some possible alternative solutions to

address the identified problem.
3. Further discuss and evaluate the alternative solutions identified.
4. Come to an agreement on the best solution acceptable to both parties.
5. Implement the agreed-upon solution.
6. Frequently evaluate how the agreed solution is working.
7. If the solution is not working, go back to number one and discuss the entire six steps.

Anger Management

It is extremely important that fathers, as well as mothers, have a basic understanding of and ways to manage anger if it is a problem. Anger is a natural but potentially powerful emotion that all of us will feel from time to time. It is important for all individuals to understand anger and appropriate ways to handle it. Expressing your anger in appropriate ways can be helpful to you to relieve stress and to express feelings you may have been keeping inside. Expressing your feelings in an appropriate and calm manner can help you see your problem from another perspective and hopefully address it in a positive manner. If you refuse to express your feelings and build up anger, eventually it will come out in an inappropriate manner that can be harmful to you and others. Some of the known causes of anger can include disappointments, unforgiveness, frustrations, hurts, and more.

When you become angry or begin to get angry, you need to take note of the changes that begin to occur in your body. If you are aware of these physical changes, it could assist you to calm yourself down or remove yourself from the situation until you can appropriately deal with your angry feelings. Some of the reactions that occur in your body include the following:

• Adrenaline and other chemicals enter the bloodstream
• The heart pumps faster
• Blood pressure rises
• Muscles tense
• Hands shake

In reality, your body is preparing for an attack, and it is important for you to recognize these changes and address them appropriately. There are occasions when anger is appropriate and can be helpful in responding to emergencies where you will get the necessary strength and courage to handle the situation in an appropriate manner. It is well known that when anger is not addressed in an appropriate manner, it can result in serious health challenges, like the following:

- High blood pressure
- Headaches
- Strokes
- Stomach problems
- Skin disorders
- Constipation or diarrhea
- Weight problems
- Other illnesses

When an individual experiences a high level of anger that is not addressed appropriately, it can be a major contributing factor to other emotional illnesses, like depression and anxiety. In interpersonal relationships, we all have probably known, experienced or heard of incidents where anger has resulted in blaming, criticism, name calling, emotional or physical abuse and unfortunately death. The Channing L. Bete Co. Inc. provides additional helpful information about this issue as well as other important information like mental illness, stress management, and so forth. They recommend the following ways to appropriately address anger.

Ways To Keep Your Anger Under Control

- **Recognize your anger.** It is a natural human emotion, so there is no need to feel ashamed or guilty. You must pay attention to the physical and emotional signs of hidden anger. These signs can include the following:
  - Tense muscles
  - Being accident-prone
  - Feelings of frustration or disappointment
  - Criticism
  - Negative self-talk
- **Try to identify the cause.** You must spend some quality time alone, thinking honestly about why you are angry. Frequently, the cause may not come to you immediately; however, it is important to spend some time thinking about it.
- **You must decide what to do to resolve the anger.** Take positive steps to resolve the problem that caused your anger.

Openly and honestly discuss the problem and your feelings, and by all means try not to let angry feelings linger.

Control Your Feelings and Emotions When Expressing Your Anger

Follow these "do's"

- **Do calm down before you discuss the issues**. You should discuss the problem when you are in a relaxed mood and present your concerns in a non-threatening and calm manner. Avoid participating in shouting matches, using profanity, and not really listening to each other.

- **Do understand your motives before you express your anger**. Evaluate whether you are trying to defeat the person and striving for a win-lose solution or are you trying to solve the problem with the goal of a win-win solution for both parties?

- **Do seek help** if you have trouble expressing your anger constructively, if you get angry too often, or if you frequently participate in non-constructive conflict and angry confrontations. It is helpful to discuss your concerns and problem with a trusted friend, colleague, or relative. At times, it may be necessary to seek a counselor for professional intervention.

Avoid These "Don't's"

- **Don't get personal** and resort to insults, use of profanity, bringing up the past, and name-calling. These methods only cause more anger and resentment.
- **Don't make accusations** you'll be sorry about later. Listen carefully to what the other person has to say and realize that there are two points of view to a problem (yours and the person you are having a confrontation with) before you draw any conclusions. You should spend time allowing the other person to express their feelings about the issue.
- **Don't avoid the issue** and hide what you truly believe. Be willing to express your opinion in a direct manner. You should always

avoid getting into physical or violent situations.

- **Don't give the silent treatment.** Avoiding discussing the problem only leads to further conflict and tension. This will not solve the problem. You must strive for an open and honest discussion of the issues at all times.

Other Ways to Control Your Temper

When you are beginning to feel angry try the following:

- **Humor**
- **Physical Activity**
- **Rest And Relaxation**
- **Pray**
- **Hobbies**
- **Time Out**

When Someone Else Is Getting Angry, Do The Following:

- **Keep your cool.** Don't answer anger with anger. Avoid yelling, throwing things, using insults, and so forth. Also avoid making statements that you will regret later.
- **Be considerate.** If others are around, encourage the angry person to discuss his or her anger privately.
- **Be a good listener.** Give the angry person your undivided attention. Use active listening skills with frequent comments to let the person know that you hear what he is saying. Frequently, angry people just need someone to listen to them and are not looking for you to solve their problem.
- **Consider the cause of the anger.** Frequently, when a person is angry, the origin of the anger may come from various experiences and circumstances.
- **Don't take chances.** Occasionally, anger can lead to violence. Always evaluate your safety and, if it appears to be threatened, you should seek assistance immediately.

The Issue Of Domestic Violence in Relationships

Under no circumstances should domestic violence be a part of any relationship. Unfortunately, there have been an increasing number of couples involved in domestic violence situations where the woman, and sometimes the man, has been physically abused by a partner. The estimated range of violence against women from a current or former spouse or boyfriend per year is from 960,000 to three million. Intimate partner violence is primarily a crime against women. In 2001, women accounted for 85 percent of the victims of intimate partner violence (588,490 total) and men accounted for approximately 15 percent of the victims (103,200 total). Although women are more likely than men to report suffering severe physical assaults from an intimate partner, there have been an increasing number of men who report being physically abused by their female partner. Frequently, incidents of domestic violence go unreported by men to agencies serving domestic violence victims. As a group facilitator and sometimes co-facilitator of men and couples groups, I can attest that it is frequently reported by the men that they have been and sometimes continue to be physically abused by their parenting partner or spouse. This abuse also includes destroying personal property belonging to the man like music CDs, videos, video games, and clothing.

It is estimated that, on average, more than three women are murdered by their husbands or boyfriends in the country every day. In 2000, 1,247 women were killed by an intimate partner and in the same year, 400 men were killed by an intimate partner. Incidents of domestic violence have included a woman being burned after her former boyfriend threw gasoline on her and set her on fire. In this particular case, there was a former and existing restraining order to keep the man away from the women but it did not prevent him from attacking her at her place of employment.

In another situation, a woman was strangled to death by her husband in her home when he came to pick up the children for an authorized weekend visit. This couple was separated during this unfortunate incident. These are just examples of the many incidents where relationships between a man and a women who, at one point, had a romantic relationship but it turned to physical violence. Again, violence against your spouse, significant other, or parenting partner should not be tolerated and has no place in a relationship. Intervention to address the potential of violence should be addressed immediately.

Another important factor about the issues of domestic violence in a home is its impact on children. Research has noted that children who are exposed to domestic violence are more likely to exhibit behavioral and physical health problems including depression, anxiety, and violence towards peers. They are also more likely to attempt suicide, abuse drugs and alcohol, run away from home, engage in teenage prostitution, and commit sexual assault crimes. You should also be aware that men, who as children were exposed to their parents' domestic violence, are twice as likely to abuse their own wives, than sons of nonviolent parents. Remember, domestic violence has a negative impact not only on the adults but also on the children. Often, children have received injuries during violent confrontations between their parents or adult caregivers. Domestic violence has no place in any relationship.

To reemphasize some information noted earlier, the following is based on information noted by the Los Angeles Commission on Assault Against Women (1995), concerning rules that should be adhered to when having a confrontation:

1. Identify the problem to be discussed and only deal with one problem at time.
2. Maintain the focus on the problem and not the person.
3. Each individual involved in the identified problem should take responsibility for their actions.
4. It is important not to bring up the past or other examples of similar problems.
5. Use "I" statements. Do not use statements than begin with "You." State how you feel.
6. You must not use put-downs, blaming, shouting, name-calling or an unpleasant tone of voice when addressing the problem.
7. You must be committed to resolving the problem.
8. If you are not satisfied with the outcome, be honest and willing to talk about the problem more.
9. Be willing to be wrong. Always try to see the problem from your partner's point of view. You must strive for a win-win solution to the problem.
10. Make sure you bring the problem up for discussion when your partner would be most receptive.
11. If the discussion is getting out of control and escalating, let your partner know you need a break but set a time when you will get back together to continue discussing the issue without getting upset.
12. It is important to listen to your partner using active listening skills. Look directly in the eyes of your partner and do not look at the paper, t.v. or other distractions. Focus on what he or she is saying and not on what you plan to say in response to the statements.

13.   Always be willing to effectively strive for COMPROMISE.

Remember, conflict is not always bad. It can be very beneficial to a relationship. If you find that it is difficult to discuss an issue, sometimes it may be because the stress level is too high or the issue is too difficult to discuss without becoming angry or defensive. Agree to take a break to calm down, but agree upon a time when you both will resume the discussion in a calm, non-confrontational, and supporting manner. Remember the goal is to resolve conflict in a relationship by trying to understand each other's point of view and by striving for a win-win solution and remembering to compromise.

9

Incarcerated Fathers

Unfortunately, many fathers find themselves behind bars and feel they are unable to fulfill their father role due to their incarceration. Fathers can still be involved with their children while incarcerated. I have had the experience of working with incarcerated fathers as a social worker and parole officer. My first social worker job was in a correctional facility where men residing in the facility had an indeterminate sentence and their release was solely based of their adjustment and progress made in the facility. In reality, a man could be placed in this facility with a two year original sentence and spend ten plus years there. Also, a man could be placed in this facility with a 75-year sentence and with good behavior, progress in therapy, employment and with education could be released within 3 to 5 years. Fortunately, the law that governed this facility is no longer constitutional. At any rate, I met a substantial number of men who desired to maintain a positive relationship with their children through visits, writing letters, and telephone calls. Although they were incarcerated, they still maintained positive contact with their children. They understood the importance of their roles as fathers although they were incarcerated. Research has noted that there is a correlation between maintaining contact with family, especially children, and low recidivism rates. There has been an increase in the number of programs targeting incarcerated fathers that assist them in maintaining contact with their children and developing skills to be involved, committed, and responsible fathers.

The National Fatherhood Initiative noted the following twelve ways to build a strong relationship with your child even though you are incarcerated:

1. **Become an Expert in Your Children and Their Stages of Growth:** You need to know what your children are learning in school and what difficulties they are facing. Incarcerated fathers should use the prison library and find the needed material to better understand the growth and development of children their child's age.

2. **Notice What Your Children Like:** You need to know what subjects your children like and talk with them about these subjects. You can get material on your children's favorite subjects and learn along with them.

3. **Respect Your Children's Mother:** It is extremely important that you maintain a good relationship with your child's mother, regardless of if you are married or not and regardless of whether you are involved in a romantic relationship with her. Showing respect for your children's mother benefits the children and helps create an emotionally supporting environment.

4. **Become a Long Distance Coach:** If your child enjoys a particular sport, learn all you can about it. When you stay on top of what is happening in your child's favorite sport, then you can share more during you contact with you child (letters, phone call and visits).

5. **Take Care of Your Own Health:** How well you take care of yourself today will determine whether your will be around in years to come. You should want to see you children grow up to be responsible adults and interact with your grand and possible your great-grandchildren. You should work out, eat the right kinds of food in moderation and do other healthy things as often as you can. Do it not only for yourself, but also for your children.

6. **Be Willing to Take Risks for Your Children:** Most men, especially incarcerated fathers, frequently find it hard to show emotions. Men are socialized not to display their emotions but to be strong and to believe that showing emotions is for women and not men. We know that is inaccurate. Men should be encouraged to display their emotions. It is healthy to express your deepest feelings to a trusted person. To help your kids grow emotionally, you must risk opening up and showing your love during phone calls, visits, and in letters. Kids can get used to physical distance but they have problems with emotional distance. Emotional distance by a father hurts kids and could possibly lead to problems when they're adults.

7. **Tell Your Children That You Love and Accept Them No Matter What:** Fathers should think about how they talk with their kids. Remember everything you say or write shows how you feel. Also your non-verbal communications (body movements, facial expressions and tone of voice) tell your children how you feel. When kids think that a parent is down on them, they start to

feel unwanted. They also try to win back the love and approval they feel they have lost. If kids still feel this way after years of trying to win a parent's love, they seek others to love and accept them. When this happens, children, especially girls, are more likely to get into bad relationships. Boys may be attracted to gangs and other inappropriate peer relationships.

8. **Don't Mess Around With Their Emotions:** Fathers should not use guilt, pity, or intimidation to get the mother of their children, your family members, or even your kids to notice you. Children learn to treat others by the way they're treated. Fathers should choose their words and actions wisely.

9. **Learn to Show Your Emotions:** Being a father means sacrifice and putting the well-being of your kids above your own. True love will draw your kids to you. You must also be open with them. One incarcerated father said it this way, "A father's love isn't shown by how many letters he gets from his kids, but by how many he sends——even when his kids don't respond."

10. **Keep the Faith:** Many incarcerated fathers find religion and spirituality a helpful support to them through troubled times. Incarcerated fathers should learn more about their own spiritual beliefs by taking advantage of books in the prison library or participating in activities and programs through their chaplain's office. Most importantly, share your spiritual and religious beliefs with your children. The lessons you have learned could help your children through the hard times they face in life.

11. **Seek Mentorship:** There are mentors available for both you and your children. Take advantage of these programs. Your counselor or chaplain may be able to help point you in the right direction. Often, faith-based and other non-profit groups will offer mentors to inmates. Mentors can help you by providing a willing ear to listen to your needs and a different perspective from your own to give you suggestions for solutions. Mentors will never replace you as a father, but can support you as you try to stay connected to your children. If your children have mentors, communicate with them often as another way to stay connected with your children.

12. **Take a Fatherhood Class:** There may be a specific program for fathering offered at your facility or it may be geared toward parenting. Sign up for these programs. The more you can learn about parents and the father's role and responsibility to his children,

the better. If your facility is not using the National Fatherhood Initiative's Inside Out Dad or another appropriate program for incarcerated fathers, suggest that they began using one.

Remember, if you are incarcerated, try to maintain a positive relationship with your children. There are programs and services available to assist you with this effort. I would encourage the mother and family members to be supportive of this positive involvement if it does not put the child or others at risk of violence or if it is determined to have other negative impact on the child and family.

Fathers and Adult Children

I have had the experience of having positive interaction with my adult sons. I can say that the fatherhood role continues after your children become adults. In reality, the adult children can be supportive and provide important insight to their father with issues he is dealing with. I have found this to be true with my sons. At times, I am giving them advice, support, and encouragement and other times they are doing the same for me. There are times when I find myself having to bring an issue to my sons that I think may eventually be detrimental to them and or their families. These issues have been discussed in a loving non-confrontational but direct and honest manner.

Overall these contacts have been a wonderful, rewarding, and sometimes challenging experience. So I am recommending that all fathers should stay positively involved with their adult children and be available to offer support, encouragement, insight, advice, or just a listening ear. At times, I have had the opportunity to give my sons advice about parenting styles that I have learned through the years. I realized they were doing some of the things they experienced me doing to them when they were younger. Some of these things included yelling and sometimes overreacting to specific situations instead of being more supportive and listening to the child's point of view. Also, avoid addressing emotionally challenging issues with children when you are tired, just getting in from work or just not in a good mood. It is important for fathers to decide when is the best time to address issues with their children (or your spouse or significant other) and put forth an effort to do it when you are in a calm mood.

I have learned that even after children reach adulthood and leave home, they will continue to look to their fathers for wisdom, advice, encouragement, and emotional support. I have also found there are times when they provide me, their father, with the same kind of support and advice. Fathers should realize their job of fathering is never over and is a very rewarding experience even after your children become adults, married and have their own families.

10

The Multi-generational Influence

Grandfathers and Grandchildren

Grandparents can play vital roles in the overall development of their grandchildren. Research has shown that grandparents often become the family's first reserve in times of crisis. Grandparents, especially the grandfather, act as fun playmates, role models, and family historians. Grandfathers can also assist in establishing self-esteem and security in their grandchildren. Some grandfathers describe their role as a nurturer and they freely show affection and a special interest in the lives of their grandchildren.

Research suggests that ignoring the existence of a grandparent who has formed a strong bond with the grandchildren may not represent the best interests of the children. A grandparent's role is an integral part of the child's self-identity. Once that relationship is established, removal of that relationship for whatever reason could result in emotional detriments to the child. In talking with several grandfathers, it is apparent that they see their roles as builders of self-esteem, nurturers and individuals who demonstrate a sincere interest in the welfare of their grandchildren and who provide guidance and support when needed. Also, let's not forget that grandfathers provide transportation for emergencies or routine trips to school, extra curricular activities, child care and medical appointments. All of these activities are great opportunities for the grandfather to spend quality time with his grandchildren and play an integral part in ensuring the continuation of the family legacy. What a wonderful and rewarding experience.

After spending the past two weeks with two and sometimes four of my grandchildren, I felt compelled to say something about the important role grandfathers play in the lives of their grandchildren. We have been blessed with four grandchildren (3 boys, ages 5, 8 and 9; and one girl, age 7).

Although exhausting at times for my wife and me, we must admit that we both had an enjoyable time. Now I am beginning to better understand why my father seemed to have so much joy whenever we brought our children to his home. He relished the chance to spend some time with them, sometimes overnight. On one occasion, my father went on vacation with my wife, our two sons and me. We traveled to Nags Head, North Carolina. Those were some precious moments, and I witnessed the happiness and joy my father had being around us, especially his grandsons.

I had an opportunity to see my father totally relaxed, happy, smiling and stress-free. He also had an opportunity to see me as a man, father and husband and appeared to be proud of the interactions I had with my family and the love we all displayed for each other. It was a very comfortable environment to function in, and we especially had fun eating dinner together and visiting some of the sights in North Carolina (Wright Brothers Museum). My father, who loved fishing, especially had an enjoyable time fishing with his grandsons and his son.

As I write about this most enjoyable experience, I realize more and more that I had an excellent example in my father, who showed me how to provide and care for a family. Although he had some difficulty openly expressing his feelings and love for his children, you felt his appreciation and love though his actions and smiles. I truly miss him. Now I better understand why he wanted to have frequent interactions with his grandchildren and the love he displayed towards them.

An effective and caring grandfather provides guidance, love, support, encouragement,, and nurturing for his grandchildren. I have been able to calmly talk to my grandchildren about the challenges they are having in school, the community, or within the family with their siblings.

Frequently, they are able to share some of their innermost feelings and fears that they may not feel comfortable sharing with their parents at the time. I try to provide them with a comfortable, supportive environment where they feel free to talk about whatever they like. I also spend some time encouraging them to be good listeners and students, to follow the instructions of their parents, and have a positive relationship with their siblings, although at times it is expected that they will experience some sibling rivalry. Other times, we just have fun times like acting silly, swimming, attending the movies, visiting the Inner Harbor in Baltimore, Maryland and the Baltimore Museum of Art, going to lunch or dinner together and playing drums and other musical instruments' together. I have had the opportunity to attend my grandsons' football, basketball and soccer practices and games. With respect to my granddaughter, I have had the opportunity to take her to dance recitals during the Christmas Holidays. She always likes to go to McDonalds following the recital. This experience has contributed to influencing her to participate in a community dance class where she is learning tap, ballet, and jazz dancing.

We have also had the opportunity to spend time together in church. Grandfathers should take advantage of every opportunity to spend quality time with their grandchildren and give them support and ask them open-ended questions so that they can express how they feel about their fears and goals. It can be an excellent time for bonding, nurturing, helping to build their positive self-esteem and helping to develop good problem solving skills that will last them a lifetime. On one occasion, I had the opportunity to spend a summer vacation with my wife, our two sons and their families, which included my two daughters-in-laws, and our four grandchildren. This was a very rewarding experience when we traveled to Myrtle Beach in South Carolina. Although I had been used to vacationing with only my wife and me, and with our children when they were younger, the Myrtle Beach experience included ten individuals (six adults and four grandchildren). This was a wonderful, rewarding, and sometimes challenging experience.

During the visit to North Carolina, we also visited one of my daughter-in-law's grandmothers in North Carolina on our way to Myrtle Beach. This was an excellent experience where we met several of her relatives. They displayed unconditional love toward all of us. I had an opportunity to observe my grandchildren interact with their adult and younger relatives, play with animals, and eat lots of excellent southern cooking. This experience reminded me of when I was very young and our family would visit my grandparents and other relatives in South Carolina during the month of August for Homecoming and Camp meeting. This gave us an opportunity to be with our grandparents and other relatives from South Carolina and Maryland.

Again, the role grandfathers play in the lives of their grandchildren can be invaluable. Grandfathers and their relationships with their grandchildren can provide a sense of security, open lines of communication, encouragement, a source of wisdom and opportunities to expand their experiences through visits to libraries, museums and nursing homes. Grandfathers should utilize every opportunity to interact with their grandchildren and assist in their healthy physical and emotional development. Grandchildren provide a sense of joy to the grandfather simply by allowing him to observe and interact with the offspring of his children.

11

The Epitome of Health

Men's Health Issues

The overall health of men continues to be a major issue facing fathers, families, and our communities. Frequently, they will not get yearly examinations or see specialists even when their physician recommends it. Also, too many men are without medical insurance, so access to medical treatment is not available in some communities. Young men will avoid going to the doctor for medical check ups unless they have a serious medical problem. This pattern of not receiving regular medical care continues as the man ages, resulting in inadequate medical care. When men do not obtain the recommended yearly physicals, it can have a negative impact on their children and families and the healthcare system. Regular physical checkups are the primary means by which men can stay healthy and monitoring their health. When visiting a doctor, men should be prepared to answer questions about their medical history like:

- Past and present health problems
- Past and current medications
- Biological family medical history (high blood pressure, heart disease, diabetes, stroke, depression, anxiety, and more.)
- Use of tobacco, drugs, alcohol, and more.

Men should also be prepared to take a blood test and urine specimen as well as checking their body from head to toe including an EKG (electrocardiogram) for signs of coronary artery disease, an enlarged heart or irregular heart rhythm. When visiting the doctor, men should be honest, open and share all medical issues and concerns they may have. It is also recommended that men write down some of their concerns and current medication in preparation for their visit to the doctor's office.

Prostate Cancer

An increasing number of men, especially African-American men, suffer from prostate problems and early examination is the key to successful evaluation and intervention as needed. The prostate gland, a key part of the male reproductive system, is linked closely with the urinary system. It is a small gland that secretes much of the liquid portion of semen, the milky fluid that transports sperm through the penis when a man ejaculates. The prostate is located just beneath the bladder, where urine is stored, and in front of the rectum. The prostate usually is healthy in younger men but as a man grows older, the prostate gland can become a source of medical problems, like inflammation, enlargement and cancer. The U.S. Department of Health and Human Services (Public Health Services, National Institutes of Health) assists men and their physicians in assessing the severity of an enlarged prostate (Benign Prostatic Hyperplasia or BPH). The American Urological Association has developed the following seven question index:

Over the past month how often have you:

- Had a sensation of not emptying you bladder completely after urinating?
- Had to urinate again less than two hours after urinating?
- Found you stopped and started again several times during urination?
- Found it difficult to postpone urination?
- Had a weak urinary stream?
- Had to push or strain to begin urination?
- Had to get up several times to urinate, from the time you went to bed at night until the time you got up in the morning (how many times)?

See the following to score your responses to the above questions. For the first six questions, give yourself the following scores:

- A score of 1 for having problems less than one time in five
- 2 for having problems less than half the time
- 3 for having problems about half the time
- 4 for having problems more than half the time
- 5 for having problems almost all the time
- For the seventh question, give yourself 1 for each time you got up in the night. (If you had to get up five times or more, use 5 for

scoring.)

Symptoms are classified as mild if your score totals 1 to 7, moderate from 8 to 19, and severe from 20 to 35.

The *Baltimore Afro-American* newspaper (10-14-06) noted, in an article by Reggie Williams, the following seven things black men should know about prostate cancer:

1. Prostate cancer is the second leading cause of death by cancer in African-American men.
2. African-American men have the highest rate of prostate cancer in the world.
3. More than 5,000 African-American men will die of the disease in 2006 and 30,770 will be diagnosed.
4. There are no noticeable symptoms during Stage I (there are four stages).
5. The chances of being diagnosed increases with each direct male relative (father, brother) who has the disease.
6. African-American men should be screened annually with a physical examination and blood work.
7. According to Dr. Richard N. Atkins, CEO of the National Prostate Cancer Coalition, the diet of African-American men - specifically red meat and fat in their diet – enhances Black men's risk of contracting the disease.

Annual physicals that include prostate screening, in addition to other recommended screenings, are highly recommended for all men but especially African-American. All men should want to stay healthy so they will be around to see their children, grandchildren and even their great-grandchildren grow up and receive the support, encouragement and wisdom they need from men.

Men and Depression

Depression is a real medical condition and, according to reports, it affects over 14 million people a year in the United States. It is believed that depression is caused by an imbalance of brain chemicals. This imbalance can happen on its own, or it can be triggered by a stressful or traumatic event in one's life. You should realize that depression can be treated successfully. If you feel you suffer from depression, it is highly recommended that you seek assistance from a qualified healthcare professional and discuss your symptoms. Some of the symptoms of depression include the following, and they may vary from person to person.

- Feeling of hopelessness
- Inability to enjoy things you previously enjoyed
- Loss of sexual desire
- Loss of self-esteem
- Irritability
- Feeling tired despite lack of activity
- Neglecting responsibilities and personal appearance
- Unresolved grief issues
- Loss of warm feelings for family and friends
- Poor concentration and indecision
- Suicidal thoughts or actions (You should get help ASAP if you or someone you know has thoughts of suicide.)

Some of the physical complaints may include:

- Lack of energy
- Sleep disturbance (too much or too little)
- Weight loss or gain
- Stomachaches, indigestion or changes in bowel habits
- Unexplained headaches or backaches

Again, if you experience any of these symptoms over a period of time, you should seek help from a medical professional for an evaluation and intervention as needed.

12

Knowing True Wisdom

A Discussion of Fatherhood with Dr. William 'Bill' Cosby

I had the pleasure and opportunity to participate as a panel member (on August, 2006) concerning a discussion of the critical and indispensable role fathers should and must play in the lives of their children. Other panel members included individuals from various community-based organizations, including social workers, clergy and psychiatrists, who have experience and expertise in working with fathers and families in the African-American community.

More importantly, the featured speaker for this event was none other than Dr. William "Bill" Cosby, educator, author, philanthropist, and actor. Coppin State University and the African-American Male Leadership Institute, both of Baltimore, Maryland, hosted this event, titled "Fatherhood Works." Dr. Cosby had visited several schools in Baltimore City earlier that day before coming to the Heritage United Church of Christ to talk about fatherhood and to call fathers to claim their children. During his school visits, he reportedly stressed the importance of education, studying and the negative messages of some lyrics of hip-hop music as well as the behavior of the hip-hop generation. He also encouraged parents to play a larger role in the lives of their children.

During an informal discussion with panel members before his presentation at the church, Bill Cosby displayed a sincere interest in the welfare of our children. He emphasized the need for parents, regardless of their relationship, to do what is required as a parent and play an active role in raising their children. He stressed that parents should be involved in their child's education by visiting schools and talking to teachers. He also emphasized that he sees children who have no pride, are sad, angry, frustrated, and feel abandoned. He discussed his contact with 8th, 9th and 10th graders in California, who were unable to describe what they were doing in specific subjects, such as math and history

Dr. Cosby also commented on the complaint from African-Americans that white America is building many new prisons. His response was, "Just because they are building more prisons, it does not mean that blacks have to go there. Stay out of the prisons!!!!" During this informal discussion, Dr. Cosby also expressed his concern that the graduation rate at Coppin State University this academic year was 80% women and 20% men. He noted that there is a need to enroll and graduate more men from higher education institutions than we are currently doing. Overall, Dr. Cosby displayed a very sincere interest in the welfare of African-Americans, especially the children. He expressed an interest in returning to Baltimore in the future, but wanted to go to the neighborhoods where the poor families with children reside and talk to and encourage them. This was a very inspirational and encouraging experience for me and the individuals who attended Dr. Cosby's presentation.

Summary

In closing, I believe absent-father homes continue to be the number one social problem facing this nation and its communities, especially the African-American community. The impact of fatherlessness can be seen in the increased crime rate, incarcerations, teenage pregnancies, violence against women, early school drop out rates, poor interpersonal relationships, mental health issues, low-self esteem, anger management, abandonment issues, and youth suicide.

At no time in history, including World War II and the Vietnam War, has father absenteeism been so high, especially in the African-American community. We need to "sound the alarm" that we are in a "state of emergency" in our communities. Our fathers need to step up to the plate and be the fathers they were ordained by God to be. Regardless of your relationship with the mother of your child, you as a parent need to fulfill your parenting roles with your children. NO MORE EXCUSES!!!!!! I realize that the role of a father has been negatively impacted by society, your relationship with your own father, individual and institutional racism, substance abuse and alcohol, mental health issues, involvement in the criminal justice system, the educational system, the social services system, and the child support enforcement system. Also, the media has historically displayed very negative images of fathers, like being unavailable, uncaring, very strict, not nurturing, and violent; however, while we must continue to address these issues, you as a father must become or continue to be a responsible, available, and committed father to your children.

Irresponsible fatherhood should not be tolerated in our families. We must begin to demand that all the men in our families who are fathers fulfill their roles and responsibilities effectively. When a father makes an attempt to be involved with his children, the mother should be supportive of these efforts, regardless of her relationship with the father. As long as the child is not at risk by being with the father, mothers should encourage that relationship. The mother's family should also support the father's involvement and not be a hindrance toward the father bonding with his child.

It is extremely important for a child to see that his parents, regardless of whether or not they are romantically involved, have a supportive, respectful and cooperative relationship. They should be in accord with the raising of the child. The father's positive involvement with his children can have a positive impact not only on this child, but also on his children's children. Parental involvement has a multi-generational impact. Positive father involvement should always be supported and encouraged.

Fathers need to believe that they can be effective fathers. They need to visualize it. A father's thoughts and expectations can have considerable influence and power on his life. Fathers need to see themselves as being positive, effective, and responsible fathers. I commend those fathers who are aware of their roles and responsibilities as fathers and are doing what is necessary to be actively involved in the lives of their children. For those who are not there yet, this is an "Emergency Call" for them to become focused and goal-directed and to obtain the needed resources required to fulfill their responsibilities as fathers. There are many resources in your community that can provide assistance to you in an effort to fulfill your responsibilities as a father. Although some communities have limited resources, individuals and agencies in your community can connect you with the services you need. You have to be persistent and determined. Please refer to the end of this book for resources on responsible fatherhood.

Keeping your family a top priority over work and other things can be challenging, but the quality time you invest in your family is immeasurable. I have the following additional recommendations for fathers and fathers-to-be:

1. Spend quality time with your children individually and together.
2. Display appreciation and support to the mother of your children.
3. Be the spiritual leader of your home and attend church and other spiritual activities with your family.
4. Get involved in your child's education by attending parents'

meetings, school activities, and conferences with teachers and administrators; volunteering at the school; and assisting with homework.

5.   Participate in the medical care of your child by making and attending doctor's appointments. Ask questions of the medical personnel if you have any concerns about the child's health or the treatment provided.

6.   Pray with and for your family daily.

7.   Keep open lines of communication between you and your children and other family members.

As stated by Richard Rowe of the African-American Male Leadership Institute, "If Not Now, When? If Not Us, Then Who?" We desperately need available, committed, and responsible fathers, actively involved in the lives of their children. This must happen now, because too many children are killed by violence, incarcerated, and become substance abusers. They suffer from mental health or behavior problems and are joining gangs at an alarming rate, and unfortunately are committing suicide at an alarming rate. We need our fathers now to save the current and future generations.

13

Fatherhood Resources

The following are the words from the CD created and produced by my son, Myles D. Barber, and this author titled "Responsible Fatherhood with Willie Barber and Friends."

Responsible   Fatherhood

Emergency, Emergency, Emergency
This is an emergency message to all fathers
regardless of age, race, religion or economic
status to become or continue to become active
responsible and committed fathers in the lives of their children.
It has been well documented that fatherlessness, a lack of responsible
fatherhood, continues to be the most significant family and social problem
facing America..
All fathers need to step up to the plate and be the
best fathers they can be for the benefit of their children, families,
communities, and this nation..
When fathers are not actively involved in the lives of their children,
the results on the child can include:

- Educational failure
- Criminal behavior
- Drug addiction
- Gang activity
- Teenage pregnancy
- Behavior problems and
- Youth suicide

The impact of fatherless homes is destroying our
children, families and communities. We must

reverse this trend now!!!!!
It has been proved that fathers play a major role
in the overall development of their children.
Responsible, active, sensitive and committed
fathers:

- Teach boys how to be men
- Assist boys in controlling aggression
- Help their children adapt to change more easily

Fathers who develop a close relationship with
their daughters:

- Produce girls with a sense of confidence
- Be their daughters first date and set the example of what a meaningful and respectful relationship should be with a man
- Provide guidance and discipline to his children
- Assist in developing respect for adults
- Help stimulate intellectual development

Some suggestions for fathers to be great fathers
include:

- Commit yourself to responsible fatherhood
- A responsible father is irreplaceable in his child's growth and development
- Believe that you have the ability to be a successful father
- Expect that once you become a father, you have begun a life time job
- Make your children a priority
- A responsible father provides love, acceptance, and recognition to the child in a way that others can not
- Provide your children with the safest and most committed family environment possible
- Spend quality uninterrupted time with your children
- Give your child undivided attention. Nothing means more to a child than attention from a parent, especially the father
- Strive to have a loving and supportive relationship with your child's mother
- Get involved in your child's school. When fathers are involved in

their child's education, including attending school meetings and volunteering at school, children are more likely to receive better grades, participate in extra curricular activities, and are less likely to repeat a grade
- Communicate positively with your children
- Be kind, gentle and loving with your words
- Love your child no matter what
- Display unconditional love toward your children. You can disapprove of their behavior and still display love and acceptance towards them
- Enjoy being a good role model for your children. Remember you are your children's first teacher and best role model
- Think about your actions and how they impact your children positively or negatively

Again this is an emergency call to all fathers to
be committed, responsible and caring fathers for
the survival of our children, families,
communities and this nation
If not us, Then who?
If not now, When?
Make a commitment to be the best father you can
be!!!!!
Emergency, Emergency, Emergency !!!!!!!!
A call for responsible, committed, available,
caring and courageous fathers
Emergency, Emergency , Emergency !!!!!!!

African-American Father's Pledge

The following is the African-American Father's Pledge, often presented by the African-American Male Leadership Institute (AAMLI), Baltimore, Maryland. It was originally developed by Haki R. Madhumbuti in his book, *Black Men: Obsolete, Single, Dangerous?* The AAMLI (Mr. Richard Rowe, President & Co-Founder, and Mr. Imam Earl El-Amin, Co-Founder) is an organization devoted to the optimal development of black men and fathers. This organization sponsors special workshops, training sessions and retreats for fathers, staff and parents.

1. I (say you name) will work to be the best father I can be.

2. I will openly display love and caring for my children.
3. I will teach by example.
4. I will read to or with my children as often as possible.
5. I will encourage and organize family activities for the home and away from home.
6. I will never be intoxicated or "high" in the presence of my children.***
7. I will never say negative or discouraging things to my children.
8. I will maintain a home that is culturally in tune with the best of African-American history, struggle and future.
9. I will teach my children to be responsible, disciplined, fair and honest.
10. As a father, I will attempt to provide my family with an atmosphere of love and security to aid them in their development into sane, loving, productive and spiritual African-Americans.
11. From this day forward, I will hold sacred my role as a father, stop making excuses, and work very hard to become the most loving, responsible, serious and committed father that I can become, because Fatherhood Works.

***On a personal note, I support this Father's Pledge; however, I must admit I have a problem with number 6 and believe that a responsible father should abstain from all uses of alcohol and other things that get him "high." Again, this is only my personal opinion.

Education is His Passport to the Future
10 Things Parents Must Do To Save Their Sons

1. Establish clear house rules about how and when homework is to be done. The most useful rule from elementary through high school is no television, video or computer games, Internet, or going outside with friends until homework is finished. It also helps to add no talking on the phone or visits from friends.
2. Be available to assist with their homework, if they need help, even if they don't understand it all. Showing an interest in their homework and making sure they get it done can make all the difference in the world.
3. Ask to see your son's completed homework. Pay attention to how much homework they are given and the quality of work your son is turning in.

4.   Praise them liberally when they do a good job (even though they are expected to do it anyway).
5.   Call your children when they are due home, if you cannot be there when they arrive from school.
6.   Arrange an after-school or Saturday homework club program with other parents for your sons.
7.   Get access to a computer. Today, most junior high and high school kids need access to a computer to do their required schoolwork and reports.
8.   Find out about community resources. Many libraries provide computers that your son may use for free after school. He may be able to access a school's computer lab during his free period, study hall or after school. Check with local churches, community centers, tutoring, or mentoring programs to see if computers are available.
9.   Ask family members, friends, neighbors, and church members to see if there is someone who can tutor your son after school if he is having trouble with his homework.
10.   Know when to "say when." If your son is an A or B high school student, seems fairly responsible and gets his work done, you may be able to give him more responsibility for his own work. Your actions should be guided by your son's performance.

(Developed by Drs. A.J. Franklin & Nancy Boyd-Franklin)
"Boys Into Men"

The Warrior Method: A Parent's Guide to Rearing Healthy Black Boys Author Dr. Raymond A. Winbush

1.   Begin at young ages to read out loud to boys about heroes and sheroes among African-Americans.
2.   Provide a broad listening repertoire to black boys that includes jazz, reggae, rhythm and blues, gospel, funk, and symphonic works by black composers.
3.   Visit museums, library exhibits and other community activities that present black history.
4.   Encourage black houses of worship to supplement your boy's education by having at least three hours of classes per week devoted to the study of black history.

5. Provide your son with films that teach the history of Africa, the period of enslavement, and its aftermath.
6. Be willing to intervene on behalf of black boys at any level to enhance their life chances.
7. Create reading groups that support black boys reading about African-American culture and life.
8. Monitor and attend school board meetings and PTA meetings.
9. Expose your sons to black businesses and set the example by supporting black businesses whenever possible.
10. Involve your son in martial arts classes and chess and debate clubs.

CHARACTERISTICS OF A GODLY MAN

- A godly man is not macho, hard, tough, womanizing or egotistical. rather he is a warrior, a mentor, a friend, and a priest. His goal is Christ likeness.
- He is a builder, nurturer, instructor, provider and protector.
- He is strong yet sensitive, firm yet tender with his children.
- He is strong yet romantic with his wife.
- He is teachable and not intimidated by the gifts and strengths in others.
- He may lead or follow on the job or church.
- He desires God above all relationships and will not compromise or turn in the face of adversity.
- The godly man's focus remains on God.
- His significant other can feel secure even though she may not totally understand how God might be leading him.
- He is following God and has the best interests of his wife and family in mind.
- He is both serious and fun-loving.
- He disciplines, protects, and loves with the same hands and heart.
- Confidence, not arrogance or boastfulness, are part of his makeup.
- His creed is integrity, and his character is unshakable.
- His word is his bond; you can trust what he says.
- Those around him become stronger because of him
- They can stand more steadily because he has helped them become spiritually strong.
- He is driven and balanced, not lazy, shiftless or impulsive.
- The godly man is accountable, first to God and then to other men and women.
- If a man will not be held accountable; he is a danger to himself and those around him.

- With spiritual maturity, the godly man walks in the fullness of God's Spirit and Word.
- He brings vision from his heart and is led by God's spirit.
- His vision is always bigger than himself and is passed on to those who come behind him.

(From "Honor Bound: *A Christian Man's Magazine* Fall 2003) Building Godly Men, Bishop Eddie Long, Senior Pastor Newbirth Missionary Baptist Church Atlanta, GA.

These words have been put to music and can be found on the CD produced by Willie Barber and his son, Myles Barber, titled "Responsible Fatherhood with Willie Barber and Friends."

The Seven Promises of a Promise Keeper

1. A Promise Keeper is committed to honor Jesus Christ through worship, prayer and obedience to God's Word through the power of the Holy Spirit.
2. A Promise Keeper is committed to pursue vital relationships with a few other men, understanding that he needs brothers to help him keep his promises.
3. A Promise Keeper is committed to practice spiritual, moral, ethical, and sexual purity.
4. A Promise Keeper is committed to build strong marriages and families through love, protection, and biblical values.
5. A Promise Keeper is committed to support the mission of his church by honoring and praying for his pastor and by actively giving his time and resources.
6. A Promise Keeper is committed to reach beyond any racial and denominational barriers to demonstrate the power of biblical unity.
7. A Promise Keeper is committed to influence this world, being obedient to the Great Commandments (Mark 12:30-31) and the Great Commission (Matthew 28:19-20).

These are the Seven Promises of the Promise Keeper men's national organization that focus on strengthening men in communities across this nation. Yearly, they hold events in several major cities where thousands of men gather to praise God and to develop the necessary tools to be effective fathers, husbands and supporters of their local churches and other places of worship.

BIBLIOGRAPHY

American Bible Society. *The Holy Bible*. New York: Contemporary English Version. American Bible Society, 1995.

Ballard, C. "Prodigal Dad." *Policy Review* 71 Winter (1995): 66-70.

Blankenhorn, D. *Fatherless America: Confronting Our Most Urgent Social Problem*. New York, NY: Harper Collins, 1996.

Blannkenhorn, D. "Where Have All the Fathers Gone: Pay, Papa, Pay." *National Review* April 3, 1995.

Brenner, E. & Horn, W. "What States are Doing to Promote Responsible Fatherhood." Washington, DC: Council of Governors' Policy Advisors. 1996

Burkett, L. "Our Fathers – Our Examples." *The Manna Good News For Delmarva*. Maranatha Inc. June 2004.

Channing L. Bete Co. Inc. *A Scriptographic Product*. South Deefield MA. 1997.

Doherty, W, E.F. Kouneski, and Erickson, M.F. *Responsible fathering: An Overview and Conceptual Framework*. St. Paul, MN: University of Minnesota, Department of Family Social Science.1996. Prepared for the U.S. Department of Health and Human Services, Office of the Assistant Secretary for Planning and Evaluation, and Administration for Children and Families.

Drew, J. *Where Were You When I Needed You Dad?* Newport Beach, CA. 1992.

Ekulona, A. *The Healthy Start Father's Journal*. Baltimore, MD: Baltimore City Healthy Start, Inc., 1996.

Gadsden, V. "The Absence of Father: Effects on Children's Development and Family Functioning." *World Without Work: Causes and Consequences of Black Male Joblessness.* Center for the Study of Social Policy and Philadelphia Children's Network. Washington, DC., Center for the Study of Social Policy. 1994

Horn, W. F. "Fathers and Welfare Reform: Making Room for Daddy." *Fatherhood Today,* 1996. 1(4), 3,7.

Johnson, D. "Father Presence Matters: A Review of the Literature." Philadelphia, PA: National Center on Fathers and Families, University of Pennsylvania, 1996.

Levene, J. A. with E.W. Pitt. *New Expectations: Community Strategies for Responsible Fatherhood.* New York, NY: Families and Work Institute, 1996.

Marzollo, J. *Fathers and Babies: How Babies Grow and What They Need from You, from Birth to 18 months.* New York: Harper Collins, 1993.

McAdoo, J. "Roles of African-American Fathers: an Ecological Perspective." *Families in Society* 74 January 1993: 28-35.

National Center on Fathers and Families. Literature review: Brief: Father presence matters: A review of the literature. Philadelphia, PA: National Center on Fathers and Families, University of Pennsylvania, 1997. Web publication: www.ncoff.gse.upenn.edu/

Ooms, T., E. Cohen and J. Hutchins. "Disconnected Dads: Strategies for Promoting Responsible Fatherhood." Family Impact Seminar. Washington, DC, 1995.

Peterson, Eugene. "The Message" *The Bible in Contemporary Language.* Colorado Springs, CO: Alive Communications, Inc., 2002.

Sorenson, Elaine. "Low- income Non-custodial Fathers Can No Longer Be Ignored." Washington, DC: Urban Institute, February 1997.

Strauss, Murray A., Richard J. Gelles, and Christine Smith *Physical Violence in American Families; Risk Factors and Adaptations to Violence in 8,145 Families.* New Brunswick: Transaction Publishers. 1990.

The Holy Bible. New York: Contemporary English Version. Bible Society, 1976.

The Holy Bible: Old and New Testaments in the King James Version. Nashville TN: Thomas Nelson Publishers 1976.

Winbush, R.A. *The Warrior Method: A Parents' Guide to Rearing Healthy Black Boys.* New York: HarperCollins Publishers, Inc., 2001.

Wolfe, D.A., C. Wekerle, D. Reitzel, and R. Gough.. "Strategies to Address Viiolence in the Lives of High Risk Youth." In Peled, E., Jaffe, P.G. and Edleson, J.L. (eds.), Ending the Cycle of Violence: Community Responses to Children of Battered Women. New York: Sage Publications. 1995.

IMPORTANT WEBSITES AND OTHER RESOURCES

- African-American Male Leadership Institute: www.aamlionline.org
- ALLPRODAD: www.allprodad.com
- Casey Family Services: www.caseyfamilyservices.com
- Center for Fathers, Families and Workforce Development (CFWD): www.cfwd.com
- Dads and Daughters: www.dadsanddaughters.org
- Great Dads: www.greatdads.org
- Institute for Responsible Fathers and Family Revitalization: http://fatherfamilylink.gse.upenn.edu/org/irf/mission.htm
- Maryland Regional Practitioners' Network for Fathers and Families (MRPNFF) 1200 West Baltimore Street Baltimore MD 21223 410-244-0751 or 1-800-859-0956. www.mrpnff.org
- MBRACEFatherhood: www.mbracefatherhood.com
- National Fatherhood Initiative: www.fatherhood.org
- National Center on Fathers and Families: www.ncoff.gse.upenn.edu
- National Center for Fathering: www.fathers.com

- National Latino Fatherhood and Family Institute (NLFFI). http://www.n;ffo.org/
- National Practitioners Network for Fathers and Families: www.npff.org
- Promise Keepers: www.promisekeepers.org
- Urban Leadership Institute: www.urbanyouth.org
- Young Fathers Responsible Fathers (Baltimore City Department of Social Services, 1900 North Howard Street Baltimore, MD 21218)   410-361-2185 http://www.dhr.state.md.us/oci/yfrfp.htm

Depression Resource Links

American Psychiatric Association
100 Wilson Blvd
Suite 1825
Arlington VA 22209-3901
(202) 682-6000
http://www.psych.org

American Psychological Association
750 First Street, N.E.
Washington, DC 20002-4242
(800) 374-2721
http://www.apa.org

Depression and Related Affective Disorders Association
Meyer 3 –181
600 North Wolf Street
Baltimore, MD 21287-7381
(410) 955-4647
http://www.drada.org

National Institute of Mental Health
NIMH Public Inquiries
6001 Executive Boulevard, Room 8184, MSC 9663
Bethesda, MD 20892-9663
(310) 443-4513
http://www.samhas.gov

Online Support Groups

Nami.org
http://www.nami.org/template.chm?section=communities

Depression and Bipolar Support Alliance
http://www.dbsalliance.org/info/OnlineSupport.html

Additional Fatherhood Resources

"Engaging Fathers: Issues and Consideration for Early Childhood Educators" (November 2002), in Young Children Vol. 57, No. 6, by Aisha Ray and Vivian Gadsden, published by the National Association for the Education of Young Children (NAEYC).

Fathers' Activities with Their Kids: Research Brief (June 2001), published by Child Trends. http:/www.childtrends.org/Files/June 2001.pdf.

"Father Involvement" (Summer 2002) Best Practice: Next Practice, by the National Child Welfare Center for Family Centered Practice.

Handbook of Father Involvement: Multidisciplinary Perspectives (2002), by Catherine S. Tamis-LeMonda and Natasha Cabrera, published by Lawrence Erlbaum Associates inc. http://www.erlbaum.com/.

Promoting Responsible Fatherhood in California: Ideas and Options (November 2002) by Jacqueline Greer and Jonathan O'Connell, Social Policy Action Network (SPAN).
http://www.spanonline.org/Calfatherhood.pdf

"Unmarried African-American Fathers' Involvement with Their Infants: The Role of Couple Relationship" (January 2004), a Fragile Families Research Brief No. 21 by the Bendheim-Thoman Center for Research on Child Wellbeing, Princeton University Social Indicators Survey Center, Columbia University. http:/crcw.princeton.edu/files/briefs/ResearchBrief21.pdf.

What Do Fathers Contribute to Children's Well-Being? (May 1999), by Child Trends, inc. http://www.childtrends.org/Files/dadchild.pdf

RESPONSIBLE FATHERHOOD PLEDGE

I pledge to be a committed, available, courageous and responsible father and maintain a supportive relationship between my children and their mother. I also pledge to strive to be the man, father and husband God has ordained me to be.

_____

Signature and Date

Acknowledgements

To God

I would like to thank God for giving me the vision for this book, as well as the music ministry. I also thank the support of my family, the musicians and others in assisting me to fulfill my visions. I pray that God will bless and put His anointing on this book as well as the music ministry so that, through the book and music, people will be drawn toward a more intimate relationship with Him and they will strive to be better fathers and obedient to His Word. I thank You, God, for Your continued blessings and the major role You play in my life and the life of my family. You are truly worthy to be praised. I also thank God for my past and current work in the areas of fathers, children and families. I pray that this book and other efforts will have a positive impact on children, fathers, families, communities and this nation. I also pray it will inspire others to pursue their dreams and their passions in life as long as they are positive and obedient to God's laws.

To My Family

Special thanks go to Shirley, my high school sweetheart, friend, helpmate, number one supporter, prayer partner, lover and wife of 40 years, for her comfort, unconditional love, support, submissiveness and commitment to me with this and all my other visions. She is truly a gift from God to me and I love, respect and cherish her so very much. I love you baby!!

Also thanks to our two sons (Noel and Myles), daughters-in-law (Aminah and Shante'), and our four wonderful grandchildren (Amyhr, Jayde, Noah and Nazaiah) for their encouragement, prayers and valuable input. I am especially proud of my two sons and the husbands that they have become. I enjoy seeing them respecting, supporting, nurturing and spending quality time with both their children and wives. Last but not least, thanks to my mother and father (Jay and Rosa Barber) and my siblings for their love and encouragement.

To My Pastor

I would like to thank my Pastor, Bishop Clifford M. Johnson, Jr., Senior Pastor of the Mt. Pleasant Church and Ministries, Baltimore, MD, for his anointed teaching and inspiration, which assist me and others in the fulfillment of our goals and visions. I also thank Bishop Johnson for allowing God to use him by ushering the congregation into the presence of God at every service. I pray that God will continue to bless him, his family and his anointed ministry.

He has always displayed a supportive, available, and concerned spirit for his congregation. He is an excellent role model as a man, father and spiritual leader of his church and community. I also enjoy his passion for not only the Word of God but for music. He is a gifted and talented singer who is able to usher the congregation into the presence of God through his singing and directing the choir and musicians. Bishop Johnson has truly been and continues to be a blessing to my family and me as well as the congregation God has entrusted to him. It is also evident that he is a blessing to his immediate and extended family members. To God Be The Glory!!!!!!

The Early Development of My Fatherhood Experiences

When I think about my early life and what has contributed to my development as a husband, father, and friend, there were many people who had a positive influence on this development. First, I give credit and all praise to God and then my parents, but especially my father, who was a hardworking, dedicated and sensitive father. He was employed as a Longshoreman and worked for over 40 years as a stevedore, loading and unloading ships in Baltimore, MD. Eventually, he became a tractor driver for Terminal Shipping Company and before his retirement, he was a checker (a job not normally held by black employees).

My father was well-respected at his place of employment and in the community. He was a person with high work ethics, who took care of his family, and "did not take any stuff off of anybody." Although he did not verbally express his love for his children frequently, you knew he loved you and cared about his family. He was a strong disciplinarian and had a look on his face that said you had better do what's right, respect others, especially adults, and not get into any trouble in school or in the community.

I can remember spending some time with him riding to Washington D. C. to visit his father, who was ill and residing with my uncle and aunt (James and Teletha Barber). My father would visit and shave his father (Jay Shannon

Barber) and check on the status of his relatives. Although we did not talk very much during these trips, they were memorable occasions. I also remember going to his place of employment and hearing his supervisor say very positive things about my father about his work ethics. My father told me that he worked hard and long hours and probably made more money than my school teachers. But he did not want me to have the same type of job and so encouraged me to get my education to better myself.

As I became an adult, my relationship with my father became more meaningful, especially after I became a father. He loved his grandchildren and would frequently call to ask how are the grandchildren and when was I going to bring them around. He would also give me advice on particular issues and eventually was able to say, when I was a married adult, how proud he was of me. Frequently, I would hear from some of his friends or other family members some positive things my father said about me, although initially he would not say those things directly to me. He was a great father, provider, nurturer, husband and friend.

As I mentioned earlier, my family and I had the wonderful experience of spending our vacation with my father in Nags Head, North Carolina. This was a very memorable experience for us all. He is truly missed, but the memories of him will last for a lifetime. I love you, Dad, and we miss you very much.

Music

As a teenager, I began my involvement in music when I witnessed a concert given by Mr. James Holliman, a music instructor and excellent community role model, at my home church, Mt. Pleasant Church and Ministries. Following the concert, Mr. Holliman invited members of the congregation who were interested in taking music lessons to contact him. Thereafter, my parents made contact with Mr. Holliman and my siblings and I began taking music lessons from him. He gave us music lessons for $0.75 to $1.50 a week and, if you did not have the money, he continued with the lessons anyway.

Mr. Holliman was an effective role model who always provided corrections and guidance while giving music lessons. He insisted that we respect each other and be prepared for our lessons. He took the band on community outings to amusements parks and other churches for concerts. He taught us about respect, high moral standards and values for successful living. Mr. Holliman was also an excellent example of a responsible father and husband. This experience also gave me an opportunity to meet other positive individuals in the community with whom I have maintained contact over the years.

Mrs. Holliman also had a major impact on the music students. She taught piano and voice, and her interactions with the students had a major influence on them and has molded them into adults with high ethical standards and values. Mr. and Mrs. Holliman were very respected in the community and their involvement with their students was a major influence on many individuals throughout the Baltimore area.

I have been blessed to have had more than 40 years of experience playing music from high school dances, orchestras, little groups, big bands, plays, musicals, special celebrations, night clubs, concert halls and, most importantly, places of worship. I have also had opportunities to meet so many positive individuals, both musicians and others, who positively contributed to my growth and experiences. I have been blessed with the opportunity to play music with local, as well as national, artists and have been able to travel and share those experiences with my family in many ways.

I am currently enjoying ministering through music in church services and at special concert performances. A great many people—too many to mention—have contributed to this ministry. I have continued to witness people being blessed by this music ministry, like musicians, congregation members and the pastors of the churches. This continues to be a very rewarding experience. I thank God for using me and others in this very special and anointed way. To God Be the Glory!!!!!!!

Church

I had an opportunity to meet and have positive interactions with many men in the church including pastors, officers, congregation members, as well as relatives. Most of these men were excellent role models and displayed effective characteristics as fathers and husbands. When necessary, they provided guidance, correction and instructions that helped mold me as an adult. The church also gave me an opportunity to develop my leadership and socialization skills and to participate in many activities within and outside of the church. The church was instrumental in developing my spiritual journey that has continued throughout my life and has benefited all with whom I have interacted, including my wife, children, friends and others. The spiritual aspect of my life has proved to be the most important impact in my development as a man, husband, father and friend. My spiritual development has enabled me to be a man with high moral and ethical standards. To God be the glory!!!!!!!

Military

When I was first drafted in the military (September 21, 1966), I thought it was the worst thing that could have happened to me, but it turned out to be most beneficial to my overall development as an adult, husband and father. I had an opportunity to travel, meet people from around the world and help produce musicals, plays and other musical activities, all without the immediate face-to-face support of my family and friends. These experiences were very positive and helped me to develop my leadership, interpersonal, social, survival and work ethic skills. They were also instrumental in maturing me to be an effective provider, husband and father. These experiences helped to develop and stabilize my relationship with my girlfriend who became my wife of forty years (God is Good!!!). Again, my military experience turned out to be one of the most beneficial experiences I have had for personal development.

Program Participants

I must say that I have been truly blessed by the individuals I have met throughout my career as a social worker, group facilitator, co-facilitator therapist, supervisor, administrator, program director and social work professor. I have met families who have been confronted with many social problems but have been able to successfully resolve those problems and maintain successful lives for themselves and their children. I have received much encouragement from the fathers in fatherhood groups that I have been fortunate enough to facilitate or co-facilitate. They have encouraged me to complete this book for them and their friends. As stated by one father in a program I was co-facilitating, "You need to complete this book for us because we need the information in the book."

I have also been encouraged by the love I have seen fathers and mothers display for their children although their living environment was challenging. They maintained their families despite many challenges. I respect and have been blessed by my work with individuals and families during my career in human services.

Although I was there to assist them in identifying their problems and assist in developing strategies for intervention, they were a blessing and encouragement to me. I pray that they are continuing to be successful in meeting their needs and the needs of their families. Also, in addition to my immediate family and friends, I have had many colleagues encourage me to complete this book and other projects in which I have been involved. Their words of encouragement and challenge have been immeasurable. God bless you all.

BIOGRAPHICAL SKETCH OF DR. WILLIE L. BARBER

Dr. Willie Barber was born and raised in East Baltimore City, Maryland, and educated in the Baltimore City Public School System. He graduated from the Paul Lawrence Dunbar High School. He also received a bachelor's degree from Morgan State University, Baltimore, MD, in Music Education and a master's degree and doctorate in Social Work from Howard University, Washington, D.C. Dr. Barber has been married for forty years to his high school sweetheart, Shirley, and is the father of two adult sons and the grandfather of three wonderful grandsons and one granddaughter.

Dr. Barber has been involved in music since he was a teenager when he began taking drum lessons and participating in a community-based orchestra directed by the late Mr. James Holliman. He continued to play music throughout high school, college, and the military. Some of the local and national artists he has performed with include Ethel Ennis, Gary Bartz, Tommy Newsom (The Tonight Show musician and arranger), jazz guitarist Kenny Burrell, Woodie Shaw, Leon Thomas, O'Donnell Levy, Arthur and Red Prysock, Webster Lewis, Paula Hatcher, Andy Bay, Winfield Parker & Praise.

In addition to his interest in and passion for music, Dr. Barber is very interested and committed to the field of human services and the "fatherhood movement." He has over 40 years of experience in the field of social work and has held such positions as social work practitioner, supervisor, administrator, statewide program director, assistant director for a social services department, professor of social work and chairman of a department of social work (Bowie State University).

In July 2003, Dr. Barber retired from his most recent teaching position in the Department of Social Work at Morgan State University to devote more time to God, his family, his music ministry, the fatherhood movement, and consultation with community-based human services organizations. He is also a member of the Music Ministry and the Marriage Ministry at the church where he grew up and was baptized as a teenager, Mt. Pleasant Church and Ministries, Baltimore, MD, where Bishop Clifford M. Johnson, Jr., is the Senior Pastor.

Originally, Dr. Barber was reluctant to share his personal information but was convinced it could inspire others to believe that with God, you can achieve whatever you want to achieve. Dr. Barber owes all he has accomplished in his life to God and the support of his family, friends and church. He is looking forward to what God has planned for him and the music ministry as well as in the fatherhood movement.

Dr. Barber has produced three CDs since retiring from Morgan State University. The first was a Gospel/Jazz CD ('Old Time Religion Plus Praise and Worship Equals Gospel Jazz with Willie Barber and Friends"" released in 2003. His second project was a CD dedicated to the responsible fatherhood movement titled "Responsible Fatherhood with Willie Barber and Friends." This CD focuses on encouraging fathers to become or continue to be responsible, accountable, available and committed to their children and families. The third CD is titled "Celebrating The Birth of Jesus With Willie Barber and Friends" All of the CDs are available by calling 410-433-0036 or by contacting CDBaby.com/willie barber1 (2 or 3).

Dr. Barber's prayer is that God will continue to use him to have a positive impact on fathers and families that will benefit children, families, the community and this nation. He also prays that God will continue to use him for the ministry of music and present concerts around Maryland and the world to minister to others and to usher them into the presence of God.

To God Be the Glory!!!!

LaVergne, TN USA
15 December 2009
167002LV00009B/5/P